THE SEA TUG ELEGIES

OF ANGELS AND WOMEN, MOSTLY

THE SEA TUG ELEGIES

OF ANGELS AND WOMEN, MOSTLY

Antonio T. de Nicolás

With a Foreword by William Packard

Paragon House
New York

First edition, 1991
Published in the United States by
Paragon House
90 Fifth Avenue
New York, NY 10011
Copyright 1990 by Antonio T. de Nicolás

Manufactured in the United States of America
10 9 8 7 6 5 4 3 2 1

Library of Congress Cataloging-in-Publication Data
De Nicolás, Antonio T., 1932–
  [The sea tug elegies]
  The sea tug elegies; & Of angels and women,
mostly: new poetry/by Antonio T. de Nicolás.
    p. cm.
  ISBN 1-55778-375-6
  I. De Nicolas, Antonio T., 1932–   Sea tug elegies.
1991. II. Title. III. Title: Of angels and women,
mostly. IV. Title: Sea tug elegies.
PS3554.E114403 1991
811'.54—dc20   90-7706
                                           CIP

Contents

Foreword

I knew Antonio de Nicolás when he was tenured Profes-
sor of Philosophy at SUNY/Stonybrook in New York where,
in this day of academic boredom and spiritual torpor, his leg-
endary lectures on the spirit of Philosophy always drew hun-
dreds of eager undergraduate students and auditors. The text
that Antonio de Nicolás developed from these courses, *Habits
of Mind: An Introduction to the Philosophy of Education* (1989,
Paragon House) is already a classic in the field, a masterful
critique of our deadwood educational system in America with
incisive remedial reading selections from the writings of Plato,
Aristotle, Aquinas, the Marquis de Sade, Voltaire, Karl Marx,
John Dewey, Ortega y Gasset, and Jacques Maritain.

Over the years I have also come to admire the translations
of Antonio de Nicolás, particularly of two important pioneer
spirits in western theology and the mystic tradition: the *spiri-
tual exercizes* of Ignatius de Loyola which de Nicolás translates
as *Powers of Imagining* (1986, State University of New York
Press); and the *Noche Oscura* of San Juan de la Cruz which de
Nicolás translates as *St. John of the Cross: Alchemist of the Soul*
(1989, Paragon House). Both these translations breathe aston-
ishing new life into traditional texts which had hitherto been
obscure, archaic, and remote to the average lay reader.

Antonio de Nicolás himself was raised in a small Spanish
village, became a student of philosophy in Poona, India, and
came to America to teach and write about philosophy and the
fiery heritage of the glorious Golden Age of Spain—that great

age of El Greco, Velasquez, Teresa de Avila, Lope de Vega, Calderon de la Barca, Cervantes, and San Juan de la Cruz.

In addition to being an inspired lecturer and translator, I can attest to Antonio de Nicolás's rare genius for conversation. I'm grateful for the talks I myself had with this amazing Platonist, especially one in which Antonio directed my attention to the awesome Myth of Er in Book Ten of the *Republic,* which describes the transmigration of souls, and is the ultimate extension of Plato's Doctrine of Recollection.

I mention these things here because I feel it is important for the reader to know who Antonio de Nicolás is before venturing on to the poems that are contained in this volume. In many of the poems that follow, Antonio de Nicolás seems to be so casual and conversational about the descent of angels or the apparitions of Paradise, and it is crucial for the reader to realize that this is no facile conceit on the part of the poet. There is nothing facile or casual about the poetry of Antonio de Nicolás, although it may seem to be so. Antonio has been strictly educated in the mystic tradition of the spiritual experience, and he knows whereof he speaks when he writes of human souls inhabited by angels; or how

> *I could count angels*
> *on the pins of her eyes.*

> *"Back Then"*

Indeed, so many of Antonio's poems deal with this fusion of Eros and angels, sexuality and spirit that it's as if he were trying to eroticize religion, or redeify Eros. And thank heaven for that, because today the schism in our psyche has grown so large we can hardly rectify it with our minds without a poet's voice to guide us back to the central mystery of Love in our lives.

Just look around us today. We can't find any authentic guidance about Love in our latest hot pop songs, or in any of our hard metal rock CD hits, or in any of our afternoon soap opera sagas of straight-arrow lives that have gone awry, or in our suburban middle class marital scenes where repression festers to such an excruciating degree.

No wonder we need a poet to show us how Eros can open us to far larger mysteries in this universe we live in.

Sappho of Lesbos in seventh century B.C. Mytelene left searing fragments from nine books of odes and elegies and hymns to tell us the crucial importance of Eros in our lives. The Roman poet Catullus (84–54 B.C.) left poems like "Vivamus Mea Lesbia" to show us the immediacy of Eros in our lives. Ovid (43 B.C.–A.D. 18) left his *Amores* and *Metamorphoses* with their stories of Eros that inspired Chaucer and Shakespeare and Marlowe. And Petronius in the *Greek Anthology* (compiled around 917 A.D.) praised the Epicurean art of Eros as the highest mystery of Love.

In modern times, poets like Robert Burns of Scotland, Robert Graves of England, Dylan Thomas of Wales, and Garcia Lorca with his dark duende spirit of Spain, similarly showed us the remorseless power of Eros in all our lives.

Now we have these poems of Antonio de Nicolás, which also remind us that human Love is an inevitable whimsical longing between man and woman which somehow reunites them to the ritual rhythms of the primal earth cycles, which is where Eros came from in the first place.

Whether Antonio's poems are frankly sexual as in "Which Angel?", where a teacher is turned on to one of his students, or in a poem like "Summer Night," where he conjures impressions:

> *waiting for breezes*
> *from the sea*
> *to release memories*
> *from ink paintings*
> *in white prisons*
>
> "*Summer Night*"

Antonio de Nicolás is, quite simply, an apostle of Eros: His angels are transformed into libidinal Heralds of Innocence.

At his best, Antonio's poems have a simple diction, mainly plain-style narrative, telling the rituals of Love:

> *to drink in memory*
> *the flowing waters*
> *of your hidden cave*
>
> "*The Descent*"

I've already mentioned Sappho and Catullus and Ovid and Petronius as great precursors of the poetry of Eros. Sometimes when I read over Antonio's endless accounts of seduction and sexuality, I like to think of him as some kind of Spanish Boccaccio, that Florentine aristocrat (1313–1375) who was a friend of Petrarch and pursued classical studies all the while witnessing the Black Death of 1348, and who wrote stories of Eros in the *Decameron,* which later inspired Chaucer and Shakespeare and Keats. For surely, Antonio de Nicolás has the same fix as Boccaccio on how sexuality pervades all manner of human experience:

> *Fra Angelico*
> *went down on his knees*
> *to steal from the sky*
> *blues and pinks*
> *and paint the intimacy of flesh*
>
> > *"Fra Angelico"*

> *to stream after stream*
> *where the lovers*
> *find in water*
> *a common bed*
> *under the parted legs*
> *of trees.*
>
> > *"The Rites of Spring"*

> *For woman is the route of all flesh,*
> *the climb on wings of light*
> *or the surrender of stone*
> *for she is the original flesh*
> *of a whole race of angels and men*
> *buried under a forest of memories*
>
> > *"Original Woman"*

Throughout the poems in this book, there is the existential immediacy of Love:

> *for this instant we now are*
> *will die*
> *if you and I*
> *do not make it memory*
>
> > *"Like a Bleeding Stag"*

I share my bed
with two women
in the same skin,
I chose one,
the other chose me,
the two never meet.

"I Share My Bed"

O, at last
to be known as one is!

"Lotus Flower and Sun"

I can hear some readers complain about these poems of Antonio de Nicolás. I can hear them say that the poems become tedious and exasperating; they get so verbose and repetitive and rhetorical; there's such an overuse of generality and abstraction and conceptualization; there are weak closures to so many of the poems; and there are too many coy recurrences of certain predictable key buzz-words like "immaculate" and "innocent" and "memories," etc.

I can also hear some readers complain about how this incredible Platonist could be so shameless as to write about a lifetime of philandering. And I can remember these are the same people who liked to complain about Robert Burns with his fair lassies, and Dylan Thomas with his drunken womanizing, and W. D. Snodgrass and Robert Lowell and Anne Sexton and Sylvia Plath who also dared to write about their first person sexuality as myth metaphor in order to penetrate the deepest mysteries of Eros.

Well, I say let these readers complain all they want to. If they like, they can always leaf ahead in this volume and read "The Poplar Tree," which achieves such a sustained lyric tone of plain-style diction and personally earned imagery, and may even be seen as some kind of monument to monogamy. Or else let these readers look at the two stunning odes, "The Pomegranàte" and "The Ear of Corn," where the poet returns to the story of Kore and Demeter, thereby returning our own sexuality to the ritual rhythms of the primal earth cycles which is where Eros originates.

No, anyone who complains of this poetry of Antonio de Nicolás' on a purely personal or prosodic level has failed to see what is going on in these poems. They are all straightforward celebrations of the first Orphic mysteries of Eros, and it took one hell of a courageous poet to bring these things to poetic form.

William Packard

THE SEA TUG
ELEGIES

For Tara who is now eleven.

TEXTUAL MEMORY

At midnight I saw the sun shine as if it were noon;
I entered the presence of the gods of the underworld
and the gods of the world above, stood near and
worshipped them from that mid region.

Apuleius in
The Golden Ass.

I.
THE POPLAR TREE

I

Stop crying, my little child,
pacing you back and forth
I have given one year of my nights
to your habit of swimming
in a woman's womb,
I held you as soon as you were born,
it is no crime, no fall,
to ascend, descend to this plane
and live as a human this stage
on the staggered journey of the light,
humans sleep when it gets dark
they wake up with the sun,
a new habit you must learn,
for nothing changes but the light
and with it what we call our life,
does the dark frighten you?
Light and dark are angels
with the power of terror or joy
but the power is not their own
they are the reflections of a larger light,
but you are more than they are
you carry the original flame
within your tiny shell of clay
your tears come from the clay
conditioned to its own death
out of its own memories of death
trying to build for itself
an immortal sheath of flesh
giving birth to the dreams of Kore
building youth for a mirror
closing herself to the outside world
within a virgin shell of dreams
condemned to live in a cave
with no gate opened to others
living only for herself,
but as soon as she forgets the flame
others steal it from her.
I am your father, but not the seed
of the flame, I am not even your trunk,

nor your soil, nor the leaves,
I, like you, am a helpless branch
shivering in the wind,
we all together make a tree
called the human species,
each of us one single branch
with the power to seed other branches
and raise similar twigs
to carry the semblance of trees
while we live our lives
with the solitude of branches
cut off from other branches
and from the tree trunk.
Do you know what we look like?
Look at the piles of bones of our mass graves
they are shaped with the semblance of trees,
bones huddled against bones
to form mountains of bones
high enough to cover the light of the sun
even the shadows of the graves
—monuments to our lack of memory—
make us believe we are real trees,
but a little wind, the slightest breeze
and the bones come apart,
they form branches around
a solid tibia or a femur,
we bury our isolation
in the dust.
Stop crying, my little child,
this dust is not for you;
do you know where you come from?
From the tug of the sea,
from the bank of all our dreams,
and from the desire of the flame
to burn the needs of the clay
by surrendering them to the fire
of the light, a fate more horrifying
to the clay than the monsters of the dark
and a desire larger than those angels creeping
through the cracks of the fears of the clay,
you carry the flame

not of the light we see,
angels, dragons, evil, devils,
but of the light with which we see,
desire of the flame
giving light to itself
in your body of clay,
you must learn to let it burn.
Do not cry, my little child,
your soil, your trunk, your seed
is not in me or in your clay,
but there, where the light originates.
Stop crying, little child,
every year, on your birthday,
the thirty-seventh day of spring,
mountains of naked virgins,
men and women all over the earth
will celebrate the memory
of the poplar tree,
pyramids of naked flesh
on the thighs and shoulders of other flesh
will build the tallest poplar tree
until it covers all the lights
of the earth and of the sun,
the prize will go to those who most resemble
the poplar tree and last longer
holding the pyramid of human flesh,
only the winners will know they were held
together by roots descending from the sky
while those who fancy themselves held by the earth
will lose,
are marionettes held only by their shoes?
Little child, you don't cry any more?
Go to sleep, stop playing with that ray of sun!

II

My little child, I have seen this poplar tree
lit with the warring lights
of the earth and of the sky
but never with the lights of the flame,
I have seen it green like moss in the sun

the rays as sharp as knives
fighting the descending ziggurats
of the red lights of the sky
and I have seen the poplar tree
with a halo of fatuous lights
neon signs of the same substance
as the human brain
pretending to have the power to kill
the individual will
and the will of the original light,
as the single leaves shiver and shake
under the lights marking the directions
of common wills or flags of war
branches are robbed of their individual light
they learn to fight like the chameleon
changing colors to fit the outside lights
until they become empty shells
with no one inside
not even the memory of a hearth
to the forgotten flame,
Hestia is dead.
My child, your grandfather
and your greatgrandfather
fought in war and both wore
the right insignias,
sang the right songs
told the same stories
of how people kill people
how they bury them
how they close them in prisons
dressed in barbed wire
away from country and home
for they belong or do not belong
to the right,
to the left,
to shades of color discordant
with those of the general group
and makes no difference if you win or lose
what is lost in the election
is regained in the battlefield

what is lost in the battlefield
is regained in the elections,
but you, my child,
remember these people
as skeletons of the flame,
faceless masks of the earth and the sky
hiding behind the skirts of the mob
trying to destroy your individual will
for the flame must not shine;
I did not join, my child,
the army or the church,
or scientists, politicians
or the healers of the soul,
I joined the band of guardians
of the flame, and this I leave
to you in testament,
that you may also live
in that middle ground
where women and gods have intercourse
and where the poplar tree shows its roots
and where I conceived you
in memory of all those dead
that traveled this same route:
your work, my work, little child,
is to keep the flame alive in you,
in me,
burning from the inside of the bark
not listening to those redeemers
who curse the branches
while stealing the light from the outside,
for the poplar tree was conceived
to stay aflame
with the power of the original light
lit in cave within cave of clay
by simply burning all that is not light
in willing surrender of flame to flame,
as it was
from the day when out of the sea
the first sperms and ova came
to mix the desires of the flame

with those of the clay
on that first lonely beach,
but the clay had been swimming
in the water of the sea
sprouting movable organs of flesh
to reach the next bend,
next round of pleasures and pain
for that first bag of skin,
the whole project was lost
when the shadow of the clay
appeared in the form of a self
to appropriate all sensation
away from the flame,
there was no home for the light,
no luminous trunk
to force the branches to dance
the silence of rainbows
when the light longing for its own reflection
let the earth unchain from the sun
and the sky break away from the sea
and matter flee
to the emptiness of space
like sheep with no shepherd and no fields
but the flame
able to gather the clay
in palpitating rows of light
after bathing it in the sea
with the dream to form one single
human race shaped as the poplar tree,
each light a spark of the flame
each on a magic carpet
each on a different flight
tracing the same arc of light
to the flaming center
at the hearth of the poplar tree
one single light lit
out of the surrender of clay
to flame, each flame retaining
its individual light
not swallowed by the original flame.

This is the tree, my child,
that guides the steps of my transit
among humans and is the path
I surrender to you
if you learn to break the limits
of Kore, Persephone and Demeter
for those of the flame,
for only the clay is witness to itself
it has windows to the outside world
it closes itself to live by its own shadow
it has organs to reach out and taste
and has the memory to chase after ghosts
held in the image of memory,
a cycle of desire opposite
to that of the flame:
the flame gives its own sensation
to the clay
it burns the images that feed the clay
it feeds the clay a dark night
of sensation until the clay grows organs
to hold the light one space above
the froth of the sea
when individual dot of life and flame
burn together as one
through the same organs of clay,
just the reverse of before,
a horrifying flow of earth and sky
burns itself through the body of clay
and impregnates the whole poplar tree
keeping alive the dreams of the branches
the pretense of imitation of the light
to give way to the concentration of an act
that fills the clay
with no expectations of results
or for whose gain,
and so the poplar tree stays lit,
at times the light is more
at times the dark is less.

III

My little child, the middle ground
is found within the cracks of time,
black holes through which the flame
gives birth in silence
to the exact sound
of a now recovered,
so do not ask the gods
to take away the sea
you need its eternal pull and tug
to stand like the sea gull
on the same moving wave
it is the space where the clay
dies for the flame
marked by the sea gull
between the straight lines
of moving waves
each movement a secret
of exact names;
the flame does not live in the sky
or on the earth
its home is one space
above the tug of the sea
the mid region of the foam
where water and air
roam towards and away from each other
where Hermes and Aphrodite
give birth to Love
two halves of the same Eros,
explosion of light
dimming all other lights
of earth and sky
as men and women burn their own clay
to let the desire of the flames
find themselves in that mid region
where all divisions find their origin.
As a child I saw this same hearth
in your greatgrandmother's home
in a large room by the kitchen
half of the room raised

above the ground to my height,
red tiles of clay spread
from wall to wall making circles
around iron grills,
this was the heart of our home
where all life was lived in winter,
women, children, a cat, a dog,
and we all played, talked, sewed
tracing the glow of the fire
with our eyes and fingers
running under the red tiles.
On this hearth I built my mid region
a movable organ of flesh
able to extend beyond the fences
of my senses of clay
destined to follow the flame;
soon I realized flame and I
had a previous engagement
like Hermes and Aphrodite
my clay was only the instrument
for the flame to chase itself,
I had done nothing for this gift
though I could still forget it.
My little child, I have tried to surprise
this same gift in you
when I see you play
with your rays of sun;
I saw once, at your age,
a red ray of sun
rest on a green leaf,
all the shadows within me
left standing, a tree of light
that has lived eternal in memory,
I used to watch the sun set
and the moon rise
but my gift would make them set and rise
within me not in the sky;
my child, have you felt sunrises
explode as on a replay
within your body of clay,
feel the moon rise to the crest

of your swelling breast
as if all life danced
within a drop of water or blood
where shapes and forms
share the motion of mist
dancing at dawn
and the light extends the feeling
large and deep
to the boundaries of the sun,
only the sun is inside
burning in the hearth of the flame
making love to its half selves
with its burning tongues?
I traveled the length of the earth
with this gift following me
as a cloud on a lonely desert
and became a stranger to my own sea
with no memories of my life among humans
though I shared with them a blind desire
of union through the flesh,
was it my own fall through the clay
or a tug of the flame?
Kore had to be raped, and I
was soon to become a man!

IV

Beware, my child, of the saviors of the soul,
like you, they stand on the hearth of the flame,
like you, they come to serve the poplar tree
to raise the flame through its veils of clay,
they have nothing to teach you
that the flame will not burn,
and those who use gods' names
do so in vain to prolong their hold
over the children of the sky or the earth,
they hold themselves wrapped
by the fatuous lights of virtue or sin;
my child, love the poplar tree,
each branch is the other home of the light
all the way to the youngest sprout,

two flames burn more than one
and have more power over the flame
when they come together in its memory
and burn in excess of each other;
your flame is not for you
but for you to light the fire
of the abused poplar tree;
though this is not what I did,
nor would Kore as long as she lives
in memory of herself and her mirror,
my child, I never wanted to share myself
with others in the plains
I reached for the side of the mountain
where eagles try their wings
mixing their feathers with fire and wind
riding the corridors of the light
while looking down on the oxen and the sheep
concerned only about my fate
and not of the poplar tree,
I tried all the mountains from the Himalayas
to the Pyrenees until suddenly
I found myself among the oxen and the sheep,
my wings folded with the surrender
of adolescence.
My child, the hubris of the human clay,
the pride of Kore to remain independent for herself,
the claim of a territory that belongs to the flame
while opening windows to the outside
to claim victims to one self
while wave after wave of turgid water
pounds to burst the walls of clay
and Kore surrenders to the color in the eye,
the moving gate, the shape of hair
framing a face with the inviting light
of a young eye,
there is no place to hide
from this storm for it comes at once
from inside and outside
either Kore is a goddess
and becomes Persephone and Demeter
or dies young at the hands

of her own image in the mirror . . .
On the wake of the storm
I made my way back to Hestia's hearth
to lick my wounds like a wounded dog
and remember the flame,
instead I found myself struggling to become
part of the things around me
listening to people the way one listens
to distant radios but these soon found
the whispering tone of the confessional,
not a hearth, a world the size of a booth,
she came out of a crowd of women
talking against the race of men
decrying the one sharing her bed
a coward who shot himself in the leg
not to fight in the war,
rivers of compassion flowed in me
with a determination in the woman to sin,
the edge of an unknown world where Kore
had no memories
only the steps of a fly
in a spider's web;
she was there, in the morning,
by my bed, the way the sea
rests upon the shore
before it breaks out in a storm,
she let the light of her eyes
rest on mine and I let her in
as my own sea rose to my mouth
pounding louder than her sin
she climbed into my bed
she slowly removed my clothes
she closed my eyes,
she must have seen some open window inside,
fear seemed to subside
as I followed the path of her fingers
all the way to the groin
as I followed her voice of command
and I wanted to go on,
but suddenly all the windows inside opened
at the same time

and what my eyes saw
was not the hearth
not even the woman
with her legs apart, or love,
but a cow belly-up . . .
My child, this is the greatest pain,
to learn that no savior can save us
from our own journey to the under world.

II.
THE POMEGRANATE

I

I raise my head, little child,
above the waters of the sea
my mouth bursting with the fruit
and the sheath of pomegranates,
red and green of pleasure and bitterness
joy and tear drops from the ruby globe
of women's wombs
the taste of blood beneath
the poppy flower
and the womb of the waters
the only path of ascent
for the clay to caress the shore
moisten the rocks
fill the turgid trees
reach the sky
searching for the water at the roots
tired of flowing in the dark
tired of filling the same veins
water in the lungs of the world
tired of the secret life of the depth
hiding under the moss of trees,
water beneath the surface of foam
water running to water
water above and below
water upon water
water with water
liquid tongue on liquid tongue
every drop a moistened mouth
making love without foam
love made rock
eternally repeating
the deep song
of the depth of water
the blood, the milk, the honey,
the salt, the taste
of pomegranates savored in the dark
until the body breaks
the tugging habit of the sea
to raise its mouth full

of red seeds and the green sheath
of pomegranates to submerge again
its lonely greed;
it is all the same
a woman, an act,
the scramble for the gate
the forced exit into the dark,
another woman, another act,
another turn of the revolving door,
no dawns in the depths of the sea,
eyes, lips, thighs multiply,
life is a continuous night,
bodies bend in surrender,
another woman, another act,
the cry of contentment,
back into the night
to bury memories and begin once more.
My child, do not blame
those making life in the dark,
they are the scapegoats
of the merchants of the light,
it is the life of Persephone
surrendering herself to no one
but following the directions of the light;
do not judge people by virtue or sin,
virtue and sin are the furniture
the merchants of the soul sell
with fear and hope,
but fear and hope steal the light
of the flame as rain steals the sun,
have you seen the flame
that springs from incense?
Curled rings of sweet smoke
choke the flame to death
with the perfumes of the soul,
virtue and sin dirty the soul
as much as fear and hope,
they cover the light for the poplar tree
not to see the flame
over the foam of the sea,
merchants advertise how the flame

ought to be, how the gods must fit
the frame of their tailor-made thoughts
and so the poplar tree is lit
with very dim lights
for the merchants need single rows
of souls individually hanging
to live for eternity
by the shadow of their own self
phosphorescence with virtues and sin
pinned to the self by their own hands;
but remember that even the salesmen
carry the flame,
save this flame,
but beware of the images they sell
for they feed the clay,
playboy, saint,
for as long as the clay may claim
stake to its own territory,
and they will protect it to the death,
except that the clay dies
while the flame finds
other bodies of clay to follow its journey
of transformation, from Kore to Persephone,
from the depth of water
to the light in the eyes.

II

Do not be surprised, my child,
life in the under world
is full of lights
for all light comes from the flame
but it is not the flame,
people smile, laugh, die in peace
content they left behind a few things
with their names or learned
how to give names to things,
it is the kind of pleasure
your tiny body feels
when muscles stretch,
tears flow, you see a face

that makes you froth;
I would have lived in the under world
but for the opacity of the clay:
to be as close to each other's flesh
as a man and a woman can,
to penetrate inside each other
to wait for the wave to submerge
their differences in a common explosion
of light
and to find one self on this side
where it all began
a man and a woman wasted
beyond all generosity
with no place else to go
all the doors to the light closed
the distance waived with a trivial gesture
a goodnight kiss
a cigarette or money for a taxi
in search of a home,
and there is no light in the dark
under the bed sheets,
all have agreed in the under world
that love is sex
a reinforcement for the clay
to keep claiming its own stake,
why do they look into each other's eyes,
the act is over with no regrets,
one of these days they might call
on one another again.
My child, look at the flame of this candle,
see how many faces it has,
blues, yellows, reds,
it is the same with the clay,
we live many lives at once,
clay being so opaque
surrenders the light
to live on its own,
the flame must break through
on its own.
We were held by the same hand
that deals out destiny

and we both met at the only place
we could close out intimacy:
two separate cars,
a woman, a man,
hand in hand through the gates
of the Hindu crematorium of the dead
in New Delhi, Lord Shiva the only eye.
When I froze she pulled me by the hand
into the burning flames all around us
rising suns and burning rainbows
around the mounds of prostrated dead
spouting fire in an exultation of death;
a mist of shimmering warm waves of air
changed the lines of the outside
into the inside of a rose
as all of life broke into a dance
of light and fire
stomping on our own bodies
with feet of molten lava
joining the burning flesh
to our own flesh
into one single landscape;
the movement was slow at first
but then it sped like spinning wheels
the axles turning the rims
in the center of her stomach
making an arc of living light
through her mouth and her thighs
letting out tiny dwarfs from the spokes
in different colors
dancing daggers of joy and pain
piercing the joined bodies
of the woman and the man
until they joined the arc of light
of the visible creatures
with diamond eyes
as they are released
from the mounds of the dead,
they stop over our bodies
as they rest on a stone with black ashes
penetrating through us

again and again
as on a parade on judgement day . . .
I discovered, my child, that clay
has its own hearth too,
between playboy and saint
abstention and chase
there is a middle way
that burns the clay
with the intense dedication of the flame.
It all depends on the perfection of the act.
We are reaching the horizons of love.

III

My child, this is a cruel fate
to live by the light of the clay
an opaque flight from dreams to ashes;
on the illusion that they belong to us
we bury our face in the dust
growing food to feed the victims
of our greedy needs
we limit the needs to the fences
of our trained senses to feed only us
while the moisture of the earth
escapes by way of sunrays,
and we stand asking from the earth
to hold still so that we may prove
our self of clay right
and we die at our own hand . . .
My child, nothing on this earth
or on the sky stands still
not even the dreams of the soul,
virtue, beauty, sin,
they flee with the tug of the sea
a rising wave creating the illusion
of virtue, beauty, sin
breaking into foam and mist
as the wave descends and breaks on
the shores of the human heart,
the stakes of the clay
die before they come to life . . .

The claims of the heart need
to be played in order to lose,
more like the chase of the light
of a candle at the rise of dawn
in the countryside,
sparks point the location
of the flame only to ride
the next wave of air as we approach . . .
My child, nothing is permanent
of what the heart claims for itself,
the clay could not have invented
a more cruel game for humans to play,
no god ever invented the appropriate sin
for such a punishment,
you play the games of love
so that you may lose
the only trophies are suffering . . .
Distrust, my child, the mouth
that promises to make you happy,
surprise instead the light of the eyes
as he performs ordinary tasks,
if the light fills the eyes
take his love
for love is all in the act
not in the consequences
(though consequences are all
that is left to measure the act).
Do not play for the results
stretch the self of clay to reach
its experienced limits
only then may you transgress
the limits of your clay.
Like a bleeding stag, my child,
I made my life
in the shade of shallow waters
cooling my burning chest
of the rage of my fencing clay
I chased the fish and ate
the bitter sweet pomegranate
and laughed at my own loneliness
wanting no one

except to steal their sweet fruit.
I was almost the barbarian
I set out to become
I measured my wisdom
by the absence of a heart
lying at night
as a fir tree by a stream
felled by the ax
hiding my bleeding heart
under the waters of the dark,
but Diana was not dead
she raised me by the hand
healing my wounds
with the living waters
of the secret mountain
returning the light to my eyes
with her own eyes
until I could face the sun
eye to eye
and cover the face of the earth
with our own flesh
and grow springs in the heart
with the drip drop of our own
liquid feeling
and dress the soil with
a mantle of our own moisture,
it was not she and I
we exchanged in love,
we managed to bend the light
to reflect its own flame
through us . . .
I have since followed this flame
through all the mountain paths
and the stars have bent their light
at the knees of my flame,
and now I am nearer to it
than she is to herself,
for I am the clay the flame needs
to know her own presence.
I saw in that woman
the secret of the temple

before it could escape
I can now live with the clay,
for even if I die by the clay
if it kills with poison all my dreams,
if my clay buries itself in the dust
or even if the flame removes her
remember it is the flame that dies,
and it is the flame put to death,
and it is the flame poisoning my dreams
and the flame wasting life
by returning dust to dust
for now I have seen the light
by seeing the flame in death, poison,
dust, wasted lives,
not as form or shape,
not as the lights we see,
but as the light with which I see,
of which the rest is only
a bent image . . .
And so the woman stays,
for in her I saw the secret
of the temple before it could escape.
My child, Hermes and Aphrodite sit
on the foam of the sea
eating pomegranates again . . .

IV

My child, I am a man,
you a little girl,
many things I don't know,
why rocks willingly bend
to be pierced by the thunder bolt
but in the end it is all the same
the need to bend the clay
to burn with the same flame of the light,
we are guardians of the flame,
our secret rests in the acts we perform,
not for whom, or why, or for what results . . .
I learned to love by making love,
no mirror can reflect the rules,

invent them or sink in the sea . . .
It was this same fear of the clay
that forced me to concentrate on
the act of love and close out the rest,
and it was this same fear
that placed my naked body
with the naked body of a woman
within this motel,
a roaring sea to our faces
a noisy road at our backs
our bodies the only line
separating the spaces of love
from the roaring trucks
and the maids trying to clean back
the habitual dust of centuries;
our bodies trapped like linen
on a clothesline
but we must make love for its own sake
a woman and a man
between a beach and a ditch
on a bed with paper thin walls
forced to protect our intimacy
with towels on the windows
instead of curtains,
but the heart insists on making love
in the only space left
by a world cursed with the rush
to drive the same road
fish on the same beach
shorten the time to be in company
and kiss out of silence
the images of the deep
desire of the heart
in a struggle to live or die
with others or alone
in a ditch by the wayside.
This is a short space,
a woman's body in length,
but all the space a warrior needs
to live or die,
and soon the lips meet

resting on each other's weight
a point of flesh
held and lightly pressed
until the point changes
from clay to liquid heat
and voices from distant waters
rush from under gates of mist
called by the rising dawn
on that point of skin,
the earth suddenly chases the fire
within the rising air
as water on water races
to the crest of the mouth
over a threshold of mortals
to a foaming sea where humans empty
each other of all the dust accumulated
under the mounds of their clay,
thus humans empty themselves of themselves
and build a world they cannot call theirs
for soon it becomes the face of
the cycles of the light
as each flame witnesses its own return
to the mirror where the gods see
their own face and where lovers
trace the image of their desire
to the flame willing its own act of love.
By the wayside, my child,
the world continues to fish and drive,
but the light is more
and the noise distant.
My child, my little girl,
I have seen the lights of
the poplar tree dim
as the sky and earth race
towards each other
and the rain extends their arms
to seal the light of the world
within their embrace
but for a woman and a man left
to cuddle on a lonely bed
as the last light is drained

and their blind hands grope in the dark
the black eyes of the woman
look at the man
desire of the clay at bay
the flesh waits with feline calm
if to pounce or lie
next to the body of the man
and they settle
for the contact of the flesh
skin against skin
pore opening to pore
clay breaking away the distances
and bending as light straws
into one single flesh.
And so they stay,
the poplar tree lit again
the blood of pomegranates mixed
with the one single nest they build
as they hold the light of the world.
My little child,
my little girl,
I must let you go
before I can hold you,
you are not of your mother
or of me
you are of the clay
and of the flame
you hold the spark of the hearth
of the flame,
you need to overcome the envy of angels
and that of death,
for you are more than the angels
they serve the secret of your birth:
the flame cannot be born without you
your origin is earlier
than your mother's womb,
but the flame cannot be born
unless you kill your parents at birth,
earlier is your birth
than the birth of the light
for you are the flame of the eye

the light of the seeing eye
and the fire to recycle
the whole earth, water, air and fire
so that the flame may see in your face
the light of its own reflection
in one single nest of light.

III.
THE EAR OF CORN

I

My little girl, you are no longer
a child, you are taller
than all my dreams,
I have seen you tend the hearth
your eyes searching for the flame
in all forms of life,
the other morning you came to me
worried face
open hands
a mound of feathers
two wired legs
a beak
dropped wings
a red stain in the neck . . .
"Dad," you said,
"if only he would sing!"
And you move on to the flame
in insects, plants, flowers
your pony, Chip . . .
Soon you will be a woman,
how can you tell them
of this flame?
The time will come for wheat to ripen,
for apples to grow red
time for waiting between grain and bread
time to celebrate the seed and the grain
within the sheath of corn
old age entering the skin
to bring harvest to the fields,
Demeter is ready for the sacrifice
while Kore has hardened with age,
Demeter is born as Kore fades
and only Demeter carries the flame.
Do not speak to others of the flame,
nor make disciples,
nor spread the word,
do not build temples,
nor form religions,
nor build monuments of memory,

nor write a gospel,
nor chant it in song,
all this is Kore's own song to herself,
you were born with the flame,
religions came after it
demanding that the dead
lie down and repent,
your flame is your life
a life without words
let your body shine to others
with the golden colors
of an ear of corn
every grain held to its
shining roots and trunk of flame,
every grain only the flesh
of water, earth, air and fire
through the mysterious exercise
of burning its own clay
from roots, seeds, soil
and ailing trunk
so it may live of the flame . . .
Stalks of corn will gather
ear after ear of flaming flesh
the only monument needed
for the resurrection of the dead.
It is not easy to become
the miracle of the ear of corn,
a religion of mysterious practice
practiced by each member of the stalk
closing all doors to outsiders
children of the earth and sky
believers in the powers of words
and the emptiness of thought,
they are looking for pomegranates
not insipid corn . . .
Above all avoid temples,
lonely mountains and caves,
your own mysteries of the hearth
to be practiced in the kitchen
for the exercise of building that space
where humans and flame

have intercourse.
The gods must have laughed
the day your mother and I
signed our life contract,
the devils must have taken a nap,
all knew I would be wax
in her Anglo-Saxon hands,
she took my land
claiming to make it a home
and buried all my gods
with all the familiar spots of the past,
she filled the empty spaces
with faces without memories for me
and filled all the corners
with foreign icons until
I lost my inside home,
she changed the will of my ancestors
for her protestant whim of laboring work
a damnation to measure space
by the quantities it held,
I became my own jailer
in my own basement
inventing by candlelight
my way back to the sun,
I started by paying bills
for things I never learned the name
— necessities or bargains—
chains to clutter the soul
without limits to what it can hold,
horses, boats, flowers, clothes,
a grocery list my soul ignored
trying to find the way out
from my Tower of London,
I wrote books till my soul ached
closed the gates of my senses of clay
to the outside world
and the world in all the rooms
of my own house,
until the gods stopped laughing,
and the devils became alert,
your mother had shaped my soul

in the discipline of a forge
stealing the foam from every wave
of the tug of the sea
and it did not matter anymore,
we gave joint birth
to you:
the whiteness of her skin,
the blue colors of her sea,
the green of her fields,
a smile with no fog or mist,
and the light of the flame
visible through all the windows
of your tiny eyes
trained in the paths of the light.
I know you will be loved as your mother is,
you will love as I do.

II

The secret of the flame,
my little girl,
is that no one has it,
the flame has itself,
it shines as a gift,
everyone carries it:
I knew this woman once
who with a brush of her lips
could give birth to a thin line
of red light
marking my inner horizon
for the sun to rise
in needles of heat
from the sand to my feet
extending my clay's skin
to where clay and flame meet
as one single human race,
how many lips did I meet in her kiss?
Whose flame flickered
at the brush of her skin?
I always felt that the living and the dead
came together at the point of her kiss.

(They told me she was a whore,
a lesbian, a free-for-all,
I never cared what she did
with her silly biography.)
A good warrior, my child,
practices the strokes of battle,
neither victory nor defeat are
as important as staying alive,
at times it feels as if the stone
may surrender the gift.
From the tallest cement tree
in Manhattan
we watch the last line
of commuting cars
head for Long Island,
a puff of smoke
coiled to the trunk
in a sudden twilight of stone,
the sounds below crawl
to a whisper of shuffling feet
the skyline is a dragon tail
in the distance
burying its feet
in the dark waters
of the East River.
A forest of cement trees
hangs in midair
our room opened
to four moons
climbing through windows
to a bed with Irish linen
a slab of cement
an altar with pale light
where human shadows are sacrificed.
Between the twilight
and the sunrise
I chased the trail
of the moons from stone
to linen to flesh
stealing from the moon
all human clearings.

I ran through four seasons
in one night
planting seeds, plowing,
pruning, building a garden
of flowers without soil,
roses without thorns
rivers without shores
storms without clouds
a dawn of white light
without sun
a sacrificial offering
to the flame
of love surrendered
without goals
a liquid fire robbed
from the stone . . .
But the sun rose
and the moons became again
frozen stones . . .

III

There is a secret will
and old Indian woman, wasted by the light,
gave me, it is older than all of us
and this is a rendering
from the original Sanskrit:
To live with walls
of fire and water
in a womb between
the earth and the sky
sharing home
with the immortal.
To enter the world
like the sun,
a ray of light
to open the space of things
separating shadows from light
the way a woman
parts her hair.
To have loins

circled by fire,
eyes made of blood and feathers,
clay that flies
on the wings of the wind
searching the directions
for excess of heat
as the flame escapes
from people and things
exchanging love
to mold gods out of the wax
of their hands
and the fire of their breath.
To ride
fire, water, wind
retracing the footsteps
of the dead, the deer,
the wild horse,
the hero, the river, the earth,
to drink poison
in individual portions of life
so that the flame may live
and resurrect with us.
To be the mirror
of every flame
and see with its own light.

IV

This, my child, is my last confession
before I return to the flame
I may have said too much,
burn it or just forget,
it is less important than you might think
all your knowledge comes from the flame,
and this is my message:
I am not offering you less
than others have,
nothing of what they have is anything
without the flame,
the flame burns the clay
but feeds on itself.

Whoever you are, my child, when you act
let it filter through your hands,
become a ghost of a thousand caves,
let the flame grow in your flame,
not as male, female, hermaphrodite,
not virgin, woman, old, young,
not chaste, harlot, shy,
but all of them at once;
let the flame kill each one
through poison, famine, sword,
let it lay her empty hands,
each will leave by a mysterious death,
but where?
Heaven, earth, fire, sea?
You will be everywhere
in none of them
and in all at once;
let him come to you
chasing the sparks of the flame,
not as husband, lover, relative, friend,
nor servant, master, hired hand,
but all at once;
let him not rise over you
as a pyramid, tomb or stone
but as a poplar tree upon a grave
without a corpse . . .
My little girl, this is the life
of the guardians of the flame,
this is the path Demeter has learned,
just follow the trail of the flame,
flowers grow, flowers die,
only the trail remains
never to be destroyed
by the salamander or the rose,
ear of corn and sun
synchronized to this trail of the flame
blossoms rest in the absence of sunrays
they open in slow surrender
from a center of moisture and blood,
wide as the sun
reaches the top of the sky

when sun and ear of corn
lift the veils of their intercourse,
blossoms close again
as the sun descends
and the ear of corn closes
its mouth with straw masks
to hide its core
from curious eyes,
and one day, my child,
this complete nakedness of the flame
will be your only dress,
—is it possible?—
your secret
will then be inside
and not outside,
as now,
within reach of a caress,
it is possible,
as my soul, my child,
has at last become synchronized
to this light and rhythm
of the hymn of the flame,
O, at last,
to be known as one is!

EPILOGUE

One buries children, one gains new children,
one dies himself; and this men take heavily,
carrying earth to earth.
But it is necessary to harvest life like
a fruit—bearing ear of corn, and that the one be,
the other not.

Euripides

OF ANGELS
AND WOMEN, MOSTLY

For my Maria,
Angel and Woman, mostly.

*". . .the sons of God came in unto the daughters
of men, and they bare children to them. . ."*

Genesis 6:4.

INTRODUCTION

Adam

If we could,
once again,
start at the beginning:
no things,
no names,
no woman, no man,
only the Flame of Paradise,
the Angel
and you and I.

The Descent of the Angel

Forests, water, sunrises,
the love of women
traveled through me
as through a large bubble of light,
clouds of sparkling dust
with the sensation of a whole season.

Flowers died at my feet
leaving in others fear
at the roots and the stem,
petals gathering in memory the pain
to attend their own funeral.

I knew life whole
with the proportions of spring,
summer, autumn, winter,
my whole skin stretched
in a dance of ritual waves
feeling life and death
with the same impunity of the gods.

I loved the whole creation
in a general embrace,
a sweeping gesture of emulation
of the love of the gods
for the world,
I ignored individual death
and the dance of desire
of the single heart
that exchanges love for death.

Why did I have to descend?
What does the individual love
of humans have
that angels and even gods
abandon the heavens
to taste its constant death?

Hermes showed me the meeting place
where angels and humans mate
by riding only the crest
of the ascending waves of the heart
and letting it dive
into its own current of water
while I hold tight to the foam
the way the sea gull holds
to the same wave
above the surface of the sea.

After that
I did not mind the descent.

The Ensnared Angel

I

He had just broken the stained windows
of the temples of the East
tired of the way they hid the light
as did the windows in the temples of the West
forcing the sun to rise
from windows and not the sky,
an empty hole filled the place of his soul
divided between the silence of the heavens
and the noise of the green earth
—he was only twenty-seven
and no woman had known him yet—;
it was time to descend to the pastures
in the plains and tend to Apollo's cows.

II

He made his way back to Spain
to lick his wounds like a wounded dog
the need to be alone in a new city
and erase all memory from the soul.

A couple befriended him,
he struggled to be part of the things
men and women talk about
the flow of individual songs against life
distant radios that soon find
the tone of the confessional,
a world the size of a booth.

III

She rode the right wavelength
complaining against men,
she hated the one sharing her bed
a coward who shot himself in the leg
not to fight in the war
and collect an officer's pension,
he hated her for not being a virgin

on their wedding day,
she had tried to overcome her frigidity
by consulting a doctor
who advised them to use a pillow
under her seat when making love
so that clitoris and penis
could have friction and that
was all right with the Church
—listen experts on Hemingway—
but she could take it no more
and thought of killing herself.

Rivers of compassion flowed
from the young man who rose
with a cloud of advice
no one cared for,
the limping officer trying to compete,
the young woman determined to transgress,
the young man caught at the edge.

"Save me, take me to your bed!"

He woke up with her
standing by his bed
her eyes bright with crime
her transparent gown
falling off her breasts,
he felt helpless like a child.

IV

She entered his bed caressing his head
slowly removing his clothes
as he closed his eyes,
fear seemed to subside
following the path of her fingers
in the dark
all the way to the groin
and her voice of command
to climb over her body and touch
to put both legs between her legs . . .

but he opened his eyes
and what he saw was not the woman
with her legs opened or love
but a cow belly-up . . .

A rage darker than the woman's whim
surged within his chest
at the fate the gods played upon him,
he still managed in ignorance
to be kind to the woman,
how much lower would they force him to descend?

He would be a witness, but never participate!

I.
OF THE WATER

Chariot of Golden Wheat

One single sail ploughing the sea,
one single sea gull diving
from the top of the mast into
the refracted rays of the sun
as if intent in the game
of drinking sunlight and not
of catching fish.
The sea gull rests on a single wave
—the same?—
claiming dominion over the whole
sea, waves flow beneath,
sun rays bend,
the whole sea waves with the grace
of a field of wheat
just before the sickle
brings it down.

That wheat was piled in mounds
over several fields
and crashed to separate husk
from grain with the weight
of a hefty wooden door,
teeth of stones,
dragged by four mules.
It was the merry-go-round
of the soul of children
—on that other shore—
riding the door with the same
majesty of the sea gull,
jumping on the wheat
at full speed, climbing back
on the speeding door to jump
once more and roll
over the stalks and into
the green field. . . .
How many sun rays did the soul
drink while lying down
face up to the sun

gathering breath
to climb again the chariot
of golden wheat!

Dusk has just come
and taken the sea gull
the way of so many memories!

It Was a Gray Day

with hanging mist
from the poplar trees
on the road
as we drove through
the barren countryside
in the North of Spain.

We stopped by a village
to refuel and were drawn
into the town's square
by the most beautiful face
on a boy,
he could not have been
more than twelve.

He watched from a distance
the games other children played
with a radiant smile
his body repeating
the movements of the game.

I approached him
as a woman came between us
and put her arms around him
looking at me
in defiance.

"Such a beautiful boy!"
I said.

"He is stupid!"
she said.
"No one will play with him.
He is all for me,
nothing to anyone else!"

"He has the most beautiful face
I have ever seen!"

"He is stupid!" She said.

At last mother and child agreed
to take a ride with me.
They sat at the back of the car.
I drove slowly through the mist.
Very soon the sun broke
through the trees,
in the rear view mirror
I could see the young boy
break into a smile,
it was pure light,
fire coming from his eyes.

Fire and light gave beauty
to the woman next to him
while my body became limp
with the peace of paradise.

(The memory of that child
followed me around the world
until I could return
five years later.

Other children were playing
in the square,
the beautiful child had died,
I could hardly recognize the mother,
she chased a child like all the others
with no fire and no light.

She looked with sadness at the car,
and looked as coarse
as the mountains,
I did not offer to take her
for a drive!)

The Truck Swerved

and hit my car
into the railing of the road
my soul knocked
at the gates of death,

the truck sped away
as a calm voice talked
from the rear of the car:

"I saw it all. He was wrong.
And you are dead right.
So am I.
Do not be deceived by my suit,
my shoes,
the color of my tweed,
I used to have wings,
I am an angel
and I almost made it,

but we angels do not live in time,
our homes are in space
waiting for a soft soul
on which we may land,
my place was this corner
of the thruway
but the souls I met
were on their way
to a fatal accident,
that left me
bouncing on the pavement
without hope of success.
Take me to the city
close to birthdays and deaths,
to the parks where people congregate
and become unguarded and soft
with room for novice angels.

In return I will shut off
the left side of your brain
and let you see on occasion the world
from the space of an angel!"

We Would Stop the Game

at the same hour every day
stand to one side
fall into sudden silence
and let him pass

we knew he had suddenly died,
his eyes were blank
his head lowered to one side
his clothes covered with dust
his hair unkept
like a fallow field

he would stand in the center of the street
raise a hand
pointing towards the cemetery:

"My angel,
my little girl!"

Back Then

when the world
was no more than an empty womb
without man or woman
and all the tombs were solid earth
and birds flew with the silence of snow
and mountains had no echo
and Paradise was as quiet
as the drop of wings,
the gods got tired of it all
and invented a new voice,

man first and then woman
and gave them flesh
to shout the feeling of the world,
not as man or woman
but as matter raised
from the depths of deafness
to the presence of the gods."

She lowered her voice
and brought her face close to mine,
I could count angels
on the pins of her eyes.

"That is why I make love."

She rubbed her naked body
against mine as she leaned over
to turn off the lights.

"I do not care what happens to me.
I must raise the human voice
over the silence of death.
This is why I must have sex
without fear of human sickness
or dying of AIDS.
By the way, what is your name?"

I drifted to sleep
and rose on my knees
to face a tribunal of gods
begging them to make the woman
stop her talk
and let me sleep.

An angel in the shape
of the shadow of a tree with light
stepped forward and explained
with the softness of a bell
that the woman in question
was a special case,
she had been for too long
the home of a neurotic angel,
would the gods consider a change?

In Their Own Image

My forefathers believed modernity
to be a notion of the devil
so they built a canal
in their own image
right in the center of the village.

The canal did not water our field
it watered those down stream,
it did not quench the thirst
of our animals
other animals drank from it,

it was a useless hole of water
circled by the fear
of children at play
and the tears of mothers
who every year surrendered
one of our own
to the monsters of the canal.

Which Angel?

San Francisco by the Bay.

She used to sit
in the front row,
her eyes as misty
as the fog,
her lips full and red
like the Golden Gate
Bridge, her body bent
forward with the sensuality
of the hills
entering the sea,
it was easy to separate
her from the other two hundred
students of philosophy,

and hear her image ring inside
with the same familiarity
of the bells of the street cars . . .
She had the appeal of an angel,
a company of feeling as clean
and sensuous as the rolling
valleys clustered with grapes.

Until one day
when she stood in front of me
with a note in her hand.

It read: "Today
I am eighteen. So,
it is now legal."

How Many Angels Can Dance?

Aristotle tried to catalogue
his garden
and devised
four necessary causes of thought
to account for everything
that was.

The Medievals tried to catalogue
the birth of God
by those same measures and came up short.
Could God be arbitrary?

The audacity of thought
to dare call the contents
of a cave
the totality of things.

The rose is measured by its color
but how does one measure the empty seed?

The soul grows wings on its own
and escapes the cave
to create without the maculate
penetration of the outside,
it gives birth to eyes
that can see the sun
outside of the cave
remember the shape of a face
not yet born
caress the sound of a voice
with no tongue or throat
touch the scent of flowers
buried in the ice of winter.

An Unnatural Act

She tells me to memorize the rules
and keep my eyes on the road
then she climbs by my side
I don wings of steel
pad my back with leather strips
and attach a wheel to my will,

suddenly the opening of the gate
the piercing at high speed
of a body of soft air,
trees, branches bend in surrender
to a will penetrating deep
into the further recesses of a womb
opening new routes
in the softness of the depth of air
waiting for a wall of flesh
to stop the flight inwards

but instead
the bending surrender of more walls
letting the will penetrate deeper
and bend, climb, descend
embraced to the whole body
of green flesh
caressing in endless waves of sensation
from the steel to the stomach
to the feet and back
to the penetration of endless moisture
at high speed.

Save My Skin

The oral message came
to save her skin
and spend the weekend
skiing in Vermont
for she was infinitely bored.

I remembered her
as a life in the outskirts,
the voice at the fringe
of any group,
the step backwards
when the group moved,
no responsibilites down the road
only a shell of skin
cultivating the ignorance
of those she called friends.

Why would she call me?
I hated skiing
but not as much as she
hated poetry.
That night I saw her in a dream.

She died and went up to heaven
begging God on her knees
to save her skin.
And this is what He did.

Two angels undressed her
pulling her skin up
from the feet to the top
of her head
in one large unbroken piece
then they cast it adrift in the sky
as fishermen cast a net on the sea

and all the angels were asked
to blow it away
from any contact with others
for eternity.

One Sleeping Angel

Three children on their way
to church have just left the door
and stepped into the stairway,
two are brothers, one a friend,
one is going to die,

the younger brother climbs
to the fifth floor
and slides at full speed
down the wax of the banister
to fall into empty space
down three floors
straight into the concrete floor
below, the older brother runs
to the stairwell to feel with his fingers
the still body lying inert
and the fingers sink
in the softness of the head
as within dough before
it becomes bread,

shouts, cries, ambulances,
the young brother ends
in the hospital
while the whole family prays
and everyone forgets
the young friend
who for hours stood still
in the same spot against the wall
at the top of the staircase,

"It was my fault,"
he was heard to whisper,
"It was my fault!"

He went home, stopped eating,
developed a fever, was put to bed,
by the time the young brother
came out of the hospital
the young friend was dead.

Those I Love

asked me to tell them my dreams,
this was my first and last:

I was young and healthy
but those I loved
wrapped me in blankets
and took me by car
to a large room in a hospital
with a doctor all white
and strapped me to a bed
without a single word
they started to take blood
from my veins.

Everyone danced around the bed
and watched the blood from my veins
flow into tube after tube
and soon the doctor left the room
and no one stopped the blood
from flowing into new tubes
and no one listened to me
and they all danced
and were happier
than when we came in
and more blood flowed
from my vein into more tubes

until this man I knew
came into the room
stopped the flow of blood
strapped the whole family
to the post of a bed
took my hand
and I knew we were going to ride
into the sunset

but by then I was awake.

The Bird

Worried face
open hands

a mound of feathers
two wired legs
a beak
dropped wings
a red stain on the neck . . .

"Dad, if only he would sing!"

Summer Night

Summer night,
silence,
body and soul
come together
to form a ring
of one
under a parasol
of lights
waiting for breezes
from the sea
to release memories
from ink paintings
in white prisons;

from the body flows
the light to see
among the shadows,
and the scent
to smell a passing god,
and the sound
to let the shadows dance,
and the taste
to savor the soul,
and the touch
to feel the hand
of the dead
join the magic ring
of flesh
and flow in veins
of poetry and song
along the shade!

If I am with the living,
where are the dead?

The Revolutionary Angel

He was the protégé of the leader
the angel of the revolution
and it was fun while in France
writing verse to keep the embers
of hope alive
and songs about the space of dreams
and of leaving waters pure
so that poets may drink downstream
and the revolution marched on
and they all made it back home.

The poet wrote of liberation
and people read him in the streets
he became famous at home
and they called him the revolutionary angel
until the leader summoned him:

"My son, with your help we won.
So, there is no more revolution now.
You must stop asking people to revolt."

But the poet still remained a poet
and read his verses in the street
the people wanted to hear him speak
but the leader silenced him
by sending him to jail
with a warning the poet did not understand,

he went back to his verses
and back to the people in the streets
and back to the palace
where the leader hugged him
and told him of his love
when they were in Paris
and how proud he was then
of the way he wrote poetry
but it was time to stop
for the benefit of the whole nation.

Soldiers took him away
in the night
with no witnesses but the dark
and shot him!

The Pact

I chased her
through the picnic grounds
though she did not know
of my chase
until we both landed
on a wild flower
by the wayside,
I like a hunter,
she like a butterfly.

We were only nine.

She held my hand:

"Flowers must live,
not be plucked!"

We made a pact,
I knew we would be friends,
but only three days later
she was dead.

Three days of vigil I spent
watching the flower by the wayside die,
flower, woman, friend were plucked
by a hand that had not
entered the pact.

II.
OF THE EARTH

O Cruel Earth

opaque flight
from dreams to ashes
revived as earth in portions
of blindness to the light
regardless of the name or the face
the same damnation
to live buried in dust
growing food
to feed new victims of the dark
that return to the earth
with the sight of the blind,

where is your moisture,
the life of animals
and plants,
where the air to fly
or the fire to burn
the track back to the earth
to die in blindness,

where the light
to mark the passages
of water to air and to fire
carrying in flight
the dust of the earth
to seed the rivers of the sky
not having to return
to this blind earth
of sin and death,

can any god find the crime
to fit this punishment?

How Sad!

Here it is,

how sad!

the secret of a woman

lying naked in the street.

How sad!

Her clothes around
her neck,
her whole body stretched,
nude shoulders,
nude breasts,
nude waist,
hair, legs . . .
her neck
turned to the side
avoiding the passers-by
and their confusion
at looking at her secrets
while ignoring
her death!

How sad!

Deception

The priest said sperm was not
a natural waste
that it had to be contained
for procreation.

We thought how lucky women were
not to be born with sperm
and how puberty
had cut us off from the freedom
to grow up like a tree
in the silent company
of the fluids of intimacy

and here we were
lined up against the wall
to be shot cleanly
by the word of God.

The body had inflamed suddenly
with the heat of the sky in summer
clouds threatened devastating storms
the soul found a hole
under the bed sheets
waiting for the storm to pass
the body might have burst
but for the soothing rain
while asleep . . .
And the storm returned
with the precision of a clock
every week
and there was more unprovoked rain.

What would happen to the earth
if rain fell only on those seeds
that grow food?

The Hand of Nikita Khrushchev

In New Delhi I became the guest
for one evening
—Russia and Spain were not then
on diplomatic speaking terms—
of the Russian Embassy
to shake the hand of Nikita Khrushchev.

My soul is tactile to the core
it hates the coarseness of chalk
and the feel of dirt lingering
in the fingers, it is at home
with the softness of skin
and the wings of the written page.

He was such a short man
flanked by a legion of other men
all dressed in black
—a funeral back home at the farm—
as the line of guests meandered
towards the smiling man at the end.

It was my turn,
the interpretor's and his head
leaned towards each other
like two blades,
I saw the smiling peasant face
and then looked into his eyes,
there I saw the earth of the farm
and felt the dirt in my hand
as his held mine,
his other free hand came on top
of both with the coarseness of chalk.

I cringed, he smiled,
I left the line.

Grandmother

would gather all the children
around the fireplace in the kitchen
and tell us bedtime stories
while adding extra logs to raise the flames
and make time for the warm air
to travel through the house
to the upstairs rooms
where the family slept.

Tonight's story is about a young woman
who had made a pact with the devil:
undying beauty for her eternal soul,
and she lived in the village
many, many years ago.

(Tall shadows, long flames!)

She got her wish on condition
she never looked at a mirror again.
How would she know her own looks?
From other women who would steal
her good looks from her.
What would happen if she looked
into a mirror?
Her soul would return
but her face and her body
would become uglier than before,
forgotten by every child, woman and man.

The village became more beautiful day by day,
she did not need mirrors,
her beauty was in every face.
But was she happy?
How could she be?
Her soul had left her,
her body felt like the face in the mirror
cold to the touch, the eye, the soul,
and it was so white, and delicate

with the colors of the lilies,
soft like the petals of a rose
but her eyes were as cold as knives,
people kept their distance.

The women of the village were in great demand
their beauty had become legend
and men came from far to marry them
and took them away.
But no one came for her,
she had no suitors,
could she bring to her wedding
only her face?

One day she took her clothes to the river
to wash, and on the mirror of the waters
she saw her beautiful face,
more beautiful than she had ever dreamt,
but she could not see her soul
and cried, and looked again
and cried even more,
at last she left
but her face remained
in the water face up.

No one in the village noticed the change,
least of all the men, they ignored her.
Some say she spent her nights
walking down to the river
talking to the waters,
others say she could not stand the loneliness
and drowned herself. The fact is
no one saw her again.

We waited for the moral of the story,
the flames were rising higher
and there was more light
than shadows.

Mirrors are only to be kept clean
and free of dust.

The Exterminating Angel

At birth he was one of us,
the same village in Spain,
the same schools,
similar families of land owners,
same past and the same future,

but he was never like any of us,
always brooding,
always dissatisfied,
his anger turned against animals,
the stupidity of his pet snake,
the smaller size of his cucumbers,
his vineyard was the only one
without muscatel grapes,

he was always on someone else's trail
building a path of resentment
on any one's success,
it was rumored he could not cast
his own physical shadow
his body was the projection
of everyone else's.

He was always at the corner
of other people's success
to remind them it had been luck
or their parents' influence
and this habit did not change
with age.

I was not surprised when he arrived
in India with a wife and son
and came to visit me at the Embassy
to inform me he was dealing
in animal guts and soon
he would become rich and
the village's most important son.

He called a few months later
with a change in plans
his son had become suddenly ill
he had to leave immediately,
nothing serious, it would go away
with rest and the fresh air
of our village in Spain.
I sensed a plea in his voice
as if he knew something
I should have known.
I had to be wrong, it was too late
to read in him signs of humanity.

The next time I heard of him
was through the newspapers
and the official mail at the Embassy.

While in India his son
had come down with smallpox,
the father thought it would go away
if they kept it hidden
from the authorities
and tucked the son away
in the village in Spain.

Instead, within three months
his son and thirty-two children
were dead.

Fra Angelico

went down on his knees
to steal from the sky
blues and pinks
and paint the intimacy of flesh
through angels and a young mother,
herself almost a child,
who conceived outside
the bonds of matrimony.

Her child became a god
the world again restored
to the original order
of love
through the defiant act
of love of a child.

I no longer need to imagine
or see the painting on the wall
you came along
child in arms
the blues and pinks of the sky
in your cheeks
the white of clouds
in your skin
pools of deep nights
in your eyes,
defiance of love
made living flesh again
in your arms
without destroying
or staining
the most intimate sky.

A Woman's Confession

I know I am possessed.

At first, I thought, this was my way
of taming men.
Until this writer came.
He was so young, so sensitive,
but he only wanted to write verse.

Poor fool. He was so easily seduced.
One single phrase
and he was conditioned
to do the rest.
He was hooked by the serious story:

"Marry me, you have taken my virginity."

Then I tried: "This is your son."

He believed us both.
He stopped writing verse
and found a real job.
It was easy after that
to break his soul.
Rumors about my affairs,
tips on the telephone to follow
my trail to every motel,
then I turned around and left
with the child while he hung
between lawyers and hell.
Legal papers or men stopped him
from seeing us.
He begged from door to door,
I had him hooked by the soul.
He fled to other continents,
not far enough from the telephone,
I dropped a simple phrase
and continued holding his soul.
After a while his unknown son

took over for me. I relaxed,
I thought I had him,
but I was wrong.
The stupid man had never stopped
writing verse.
It had the quality of the best,
I felt betrayed,
someone else had taken hold of me
to stop him from writing poetry,
and both had lost.

I had one last ace up my sleeve,
to tell the stupid poet and his son
the whole truth,
this should bring his soul back,
for awhile!

A Poet's Confession

I cannot close my soul
to winter and open it up
only to autumn, summer and spring.
My soul lives in fire,
light, water, earth and wind.
Like them I carry no names,
things or stories belonging
to other people, angels
or even gods, much less my own.
I cannot be tied down
to other creatures' wills.
Death filters through my skin.
This is my chosen vocation
with no protection from humans,
angels or gods.

I am the original voice
of human life, I mark the path
of passage, I am the corner
death turns to wear the masks
of new life, named, counted, revived,
made visible in the spring of the world.
I am the revolving door
of all the winters of the soul!

Skin

I looked at you
as you undressed
and became lost
in the most magical landscape

but you made it disappear
as your fingers
pointed only at skin
surface without dreams

lips, hair, loins, breasts
with less depth
than when you let me
dress your skin with the magic
flesh of the imagination's dreams.

Let me dress you again!

I Am Listening

with my eyes
to the footprints of the dead
burning hours of light
on the shadows of the written page
with the oil of lives past
and my soul grows fainter
with the exercise
and the fear
of my own life lost.

Why not settle for the outside,
the life others make
and steal from them
the shadows of imitation?

Why lean on the shoulders
of the dead not to let memory fail
in the recreation of the original acts
that made life in the dark
and not in the imitation of the outside?

My soul is chained to the dead
learning to sail upstream
to ports of the infancy
of the human race
as distant from me
as my will is from the original
act of creation
I am trying to repeat
while my soul burns
hours of light
with the oil of past lives.

The Rites of Spring

Sky and earth
stare at each other
like two frozen lovers
caught just short of
a last embrace

until spring arrives
with a wand of light
releases the lovers
from each other
makes room for the sun
and the play of
golds, blues, mauves,
the green of life
surges through limbs
through blood
through the song of birds
at the top of trees
and descends in
intoxication beyond dreams
to stream after stream
where the lovers
find in water
a common bed
under the parted legs
of trees.

Sky and earth
at last embrace
as they tumble together
towards the sea.

O, the rites
of spring!

Play of the Gods

Heroes and gods
with their goddesses
descend in summer
to the South of Spain
to rest from the success
of their habits of perfection.

Tennis at midday
social conversation from five to five
dinner with fish and white dry wine
till the rise of dawn
a sustained ride
on a high of wit and feeling
no ordinary mortal could keep up with
intruders were kept out
of the walls of this fraternity
trained in the habits of gods.

This summer was like the rest
except for the presence of
a young local woman
at home without awe by the conversation
the gods fascinated
by her youth and beauty.

As the days went on
they talked more to her
than to the rest
they made her the flower
of their centerpiece,
the rivers of the sky overflowed,
her body by now the size
of any other body in the group,

then came the time to depart
god after god flew away
England, Germany, Madrid,
the United States,

the young woman and Hermes
the only ones left.

At five she came for the regular round
of drinks, dinner, white wine and fish,
then she made her speech:

"I am twenty-one and I am a virgin.
My fate is to live among mortals,
they will not appreciate what I have to give."

They followed the rites of other nights
to end in the balcony of his suite.
As the dawn rose
drops of blood fell from its face
upon the white marble of the sea.

The World Keeps Sending a Clown

to inform the audience
there is a fire
in the circus,
they all laugh,
they all die.

The gods did not fare better
sending one of their own,
—or so the story goes—
he died at the cross.

Necessity is the only story
that shapes the soul
like a rope around the neck
of women, children and men,
they stretch their muscles
and learn to let the air escape
pretending there is no rope

and perform each act
as if it were the last
so that fire does not start
in the basement of the soul
and no clowns or saviors
are called to save the lives
of people with masks,

they will always pretend
there is no one inside,
they will laugh,
they will all die.

Between Andheri and Bombay

the road overflows
with successive stalls
built of mud, cow-dung, tin and foil
where humans huddle
under the fate of making a life
without fear or hope,
and this Christmas Eve is the same
as any other day

a mass of flesh and bones
with the raw sexuality of animal life
a sight the eye chases and the soul hides
with the introversion of the snail,

except that across from the bus stop
a woman fills the horizon of the eye
as she struggles to grind corn
and wipes her sweat across the face
and then pulls herself up
letting the world see the drum
of her naked stomach stretched
to the last extension of pregnancy.

Naked children play around her
as if the world were a crystal bell
their voices ringing with the clarity
of early showers in May,
older women keep an eye
on the pregnant mother
her standing up a sign
to set everyone in motion,
water is poured on a copper pot
logs are thrown on a fire,
the pregnant woman leaves the corn
and enters the open door of the hut,
two girls stretch a sari over
the empty door, women come and go
behind the cloth and for a moment
all life seems to stand still,

a long silence, a muffled human yelp,
another silence, and the cry of a new voice,
the song of a newborn baby
covers the noise of the choir of crows
in the circle of trees.

No one seems to notice,
life continues as before,
the child moves around
in the arms of the women,
children continue to play,
the young mother moves the girls
and the sari from the door
she bends over the stone and
continues to grind her corn.

No candle, no song,
no angels on this road?

Intimacy Was a Painful Absence

in the presence of this woman
hiding behind the company of others
as we made our way to the Taj Mahal,

but she started to confide
in a whisper how she had come to India
to recover from the only fear she had
a snake swam towards her
in her swimming pool
and she almost drowned.

She had spent seven months
between life and death
and then another five
to set her brain straight
psychiatrists trying to convince her
that everything is a symbol
her trauma a direct sign
of her fear of men.

If everything is a symbol,
she said, then nothing is itself,
a sure way of displacing religion
from the underworld of the soul,
the way they wanted me
to release my virginity.

We had just arrived at the edge of a garden
facing a pool reflecting
the symmetrical lines
and carved spaces of the Taj Mahal,
a woman's curves and lines
poised eternally upon the grass
facing a mirror at her feet,

a woman's intimacies
in the middle of the jungle
a hand of marble extending human dreams,
stone in the mold of the love of the gods.

A man can stand on this grass
face the Taj Mahal
and feel the exuberance of stone
with the boldness of a god
breaking through doors
to feel the spaces of a woman
from the inside

hollowed rock for a man to taste
the feeling of the hand
following the lines of the empty stone
when earth, water, wind
no longer are felt at the end of a hand
that touches a woman with love.

My visiting friend
had left my side
from the moment we arrived
she was by the pool
talking to a turbanned man
pulling snakes from a basket
and he let her hold them in her hand,

suddenly she made up her mind
she picked up a medium sized boa
and let it slide down her shoulder
around her waist
and the deliberate descent
down her thigh and leg,

then she turned her face,
in her eyes I could feel
the two intimacies of stone and flesh.

The Descent

upstream
of my eyes caressing the shape
of your oval face
tracing the lines
of your round shoulders
down hills
to the lake
at the waist
in the waves and rhythms
of your flesh
and then bend
to drink in memory
the flowing waters
of your hidden cave.

The Shrine

Every village in Spain
has a shrine in the outskirts,
a place of apparitions
where hills and souls burst
with grapes, wheat and visions
where grown-ups celebrate
and children play hide and seek.

After so many years
the shrine in my village fills
my soul with fear
even in memory,

for I was only playing with her
innocent games
and suddenly I saw
a live and writhing snake
hanging from the tree
right over her head
shining as the girl laughed
not able to see it
nor did anyone else.

Why did my soul suddenly fill
with the joys of spring,
wave with the rhythm of wheat fields
intoxicate my lungs
with the warmth of wine
and dazzle my eyes
with such glorious light?

Can a snake give joy,
be an angel of light?

Why this restlessness inside?

It Became the Ritual

of that long and humid summer:
Every afternoon at three
five little girls
made their way in circles
to a watching post
behind the trees
to see in the distance
an old man shower,
stretch all naked
upon a bench in the open porch
and dry under the high sun.

There was innocence,
the silent voice
of a continuous call
of flesh leaving
and flesh entering the ring
of life, the sensuality of summer
inducting curiosity
into memory.

The girls learned to be very quiet
the old man performed
as if every move were his last
and he stretched as if in fact
he were dead,

except for the last day
before returning to school
when every move seemed more precise
as if tried before hand.

The old man is laying down
as close to death
as a last breath,
the girls look on,
serious at first
dressed in their Sunday's best
and smile at themselves.

They form a tighter circle
around the stretched body
of the old naked man,
they let their hair down
and one by one
in silence
bend over the old man
then wait for the others
and take flight together
like a surprised flock of birds.

From their watching post
they see the old man
wake and look down in astonishment
at the five red ribbons
he found hanging
from his high crotch.

A Woman's Second Door

She stood naked
dazzled by the light
her back to the river
her lips and thighs
slightly open facing
the full-length mirror
waiting like so many others
for her young love
to take her away,

instead the light in the mirror
made her die inside
as surface of light
and depth of the river
came together as a new voice
ordering her to serve
but never surrender to men
and their legacy of children.

He followed the same river's bend
from Oakdale to Greatriver
guiding his Boston whaler
through the currents of the Hudson,
he had been accepted to medical school . . .

They kissed and laughed
they would be married in style
buy a house, have children . . .
he made a mound of sand
he kissed her more
she got involved
her clothes above her waist
her hair spread over the sand
she found his hands inside her thighs
he climbed
he forced his way
she held her breath
he begun to thrust

the voice of the mirror spoke,
it froze her surrender
she raised her knees
turned him face up
he gasped gaping at his hands
with his organ bathed in moonlight.
"How far do you think you can go?"

He stood up,
cursed the woman in the dark
ran with his clothes in his hands
climbed his Boston whaler
and left swallowed by a deep fog . . .

A fishing boat rammed the Boston whaler,
the young man entered the secret
of the depth only upon his death.

The young woman entered religion
to keep her second door shut.

The Nun/Woman

The young poet was chasing
the trail of the gods
in the Indian sunset and sunrise
the young nun dedicated her life
to serve God
in a Bombay nursing home.

Fate brought them together
to cross swords with no blades
a man and a woman around the intimacies
of a bed with an appendix surrendered,

talcum powder spread
over the naked flesh
to mitigate the heat,
long hours of company
long looks of a trained nurse,
the challenge to a man
of a woman with no pretense.

Inch by inch the territory with skin
surrendered to her powdered hands,
silence could not separate
charity from caress,
live crows pick bones
of excessive flesh on the nearby
towers of Malabar Hill,
who can pick the soul as clean?

One year later
the young poet had to rest again
in the same room of the same nursing home,
the secret of the nun
a black crow in his bed
as Mother Superior spoke
of this test
every nun has to pass,
she remembered herself . . .

The young nun lived in her cell
bitter that God could change
his mind and allow her to fall
in love with a man,

"but you must see her again,
let her know her own decision.
Remember we are all friends!"

The young poet walked immaculate
corridors drenched in shade,
the young nun stood at the end
her eyes widening as he approached:

"Why didn't you do this before,
dress as a man?"

They laughed and let the shade
bring them closer.

He leaned his face
she raised hers
they closed their eyes
their lips touched
as they heard the sound
of gates closing shut.

She lowered her eyes,
he turned around and left
glad the mountains were still there!

Original Woman

(Sister Ancilla's myth)

Stars in a clear night,
grains of sand
on a scorching beach,
drops of water
on a raging sea,
knives of ice
in the frozen winter,
leaves in autumn
abandoning the trees,
dead children
buried in cemeteries

are the only memories
a woman's body has become
under the curse of stories
of the fall
a wall separating women
from an origin without death,
from flesh stretched
to be company of gods, angels
and the birth of a human race
present in her
like an ageless sun
with no death
if only women dared
to roll aside the stone
covering the entrance to their own light
and let intimacy rise
to the lips of original woman.

(The five daughters of Python
had gathered again not to tie
a ribbon on an old man's crotch
but to bury their mentor nun,
returning flesh to earth
their eyes listening

to the voice of the dead.
And they held their breath
letting the trees bend
over their secret sect,
like the trees in Paradise
witnessing the birth
of that first woman
Sister Ancilla loved:)

Not made of dust
but of the flesh of man
rivers of light
stealing the colors of the earth
stalks of wheat
running down her woman's back
the light of the stars
turned to fire
in the caves of her eyes
while her woman's flesh
rode the crest of every wave of air
filling her breasts
with fruits of joy
and her soul riding an ascending surf
on a sea without shores.

(The sky above the earth
sounded like a church bell
with the dead nun's words.)

Suddenly that first woman felt
the shiver of a stolen choice
the lust to be like God
eternal willow of light
bending the sky
in a surrender of endless water
poplar of air
filling the earth
with one single human embrace
that would never die
but reach individually
the limits of the light

with no individual death
or pain

for she knew she was the gate

of angels and gods
able to give birth
by quenching all thirst
for her breasts were the original
fountain of human thirst,
her loins the original harvest
of pleasure and birth,
her body the gates
for gods, angels and mere men
for they all drink from her,
thirst for her
are born through her
even when their memories are divided
the way ivy divides a wall
into light and shadows.

And it was her choice
to surrender her inner gate
only to the torch of the angel
under the forbidden tree,
a whole season of love
stored in her soul
as the angel drove
the fire of his flaming tree
through the loins
to the inner gate
where a woman's will
and her flesh meet
in a total surrender
that dissolves all other choices
except the need to serve mere men.

(Roses fell on the tomb of the nun,
four were white
only one red,
sacrificial love

had driven them to choose marriage
and stay virgins,
a service to men
at the outer gates
by an act of will
trained to surrender only
to the gods or angels in the flesh,
and only one had opened that gate.)

For woman is the route of all flesh,
the climb on wings of light
or the surrender of stone
for she is the original flesh
of a whole race of angels and men
buried under a forest of memories:
single trees,
grains of sand,
knives of ice,
dead children,
a wound at the center of all flesh,
a well covered with ivy,
thirst never quenched,

and also the home of memory,
a human corridor
that turns upon itself
to the starting gates
of the light knocking
at the human soul,
the bottom of a blind hole,
the still waters under the surf
and the thirst
for the spring that flows
under the human earth,
the birth
of gods, heroes, angels, men,

but only when men love her
with the will of the gods.

(The five sisters of the sect huddled
over the mound of moved earth.
Their chant had the determination
of an initiation rite.)

> *Original woman,*
> *gate of the fall*
> *and of the home of the gods.*
> *We serve time*
> *while we hold eternity*
> *in our hand.*
>
> *We are the glass,*
> *the water and the thirst.*
> *Serve your fellow man,*
> *but surrender only*
> *to angels or to God!*

III.
OF THE AIR

My Soul Had Already Brimmed

with sunsets
rolled with the magic currents of the wind
plunged with the tides of the sea
undulated with the perspective of the clouds
cried over green trees on the plains
held the birds and the butterflies on her hand
smiled with the dawn and opened to dreams
in the twilight under close eyelids, and yet
she never took flight in the light
or in the dark
until she saw an unrequested flame
in the depth of a young eye.

Like a Bleeding Stag

I made my life
in the shade of shallow waters
cooling my burning chest
of the rage of dreams
chasing the fish and laughing
at my own loneliness
wanting no one
no one wanting me.

I was almost the barbarian
I set out to be
measuring my wisdom
by the absence of a heart
lying at night
like a fir tree by a stream
felled by the ax of human wills
hiding the bleeding branches
on the silent waters of the dark,

why did you give me your hand?
Diana is dead!
You healed my wounds
with living waters
from your secret mountain
returning my legs
to the strength of the earth
raising my eyes to the light of the sky
once more facing the sun eye to eye

and I saw them all in your face
not of a woman
but of a whole world
present in your flesh,

and now that we know
it is love we own
let us make names,
cover the face of the earth

with drops of our own flesh
break open the rocks
with the drip drop of our liquid feeling
and dress the soil
with a mantle of moisture

for this instant we now are
will die
if you and I
do not make it memory
and mark the paths of the forest
with the seeds of the gods
by speaking out the word
of our own flesh
in a trail of names.

It is not you and I
we exchange in love,
we have at last bent the light
to relfect its own flame!

Let us make names!

The Consoling Angel

Who was the angel
who consoled you
in the Mount of Olives
blood streaming with your sweat
the light in your soul less
than the drops of moon rays
climbing down the branches
to the patch of grass
under your sunken body
aghast at the sudden truth
that being human is only
a stage within a staggered plan
to carry all flesh
to the transparency of the light
away from the thickness of stones,
water, earth and the shadows of thought.

But you were alone,
a man rejected by his tribe,
sold by his friends,
ignored by those you loved,
indifferent to your high call
and the urgency of your mission,
to the hope that the distant goal
made no difference
for you felt the weight
of what a man is,
the horizon of all rejections,
the indifference to good deeds,
the impossibility to feel responsibility
for the whole human race
when its members reject your effort
and point their fingers
for the authorities to kill you
and they live in peace.

Why do you feel
that theirs is the peace of the dead,

that they bury the wings of the flesh
under their feet,
that without your sacrifice
they would sink below
the level of redemption
and delay salvation
for another million years,
why do you feel
you alone could be spared
the damnation of the chosen
if you have not yet risen
or been crucified
or have a church named after you
or written Gospels
or rent the Tablets of the Temple
as you die?

Who was the angel
who consoled you
and what did she say
to make you surrender
your body to death
for your soul was in the dark
and could not understand,
nor know, or even hope
you were going to win?

How did you know you were good
when you had no sons, no wife,
no equals, no job,
nor fell in love,
and broke the law?

Who was the angel
who consoled you?

Grandfather

Grandfather divided the soul
the way the village broke
into memories of wine and milk.

Intimacy begins with a woman's milk
feeding the child at her breasts
as the child learns to love and live
with his eyes closed
pressing his fingers
as he draws memories
from the sounds outside,
laughter, song, talk,
the trot of animals on cobblestones,
the whisper of air through his lungs,
a whole life drawn into intimacy
by a will centered on the taste,
the smell, the touch of breasts and milk,
memories and dreams in the dark,
where gods and humans mix
with the softness of a woman's skin.

But wine opens the eyes
to see the human body from the outside,
an object of jest,
occasional play of sex,
as when foreigners came to the village
to harvest the grapes,

men and women chased one another
and smashed grapes on their clothes,
faces, heads, laughing as they drank,
grandfather and I watching on horseback,
as the whole town bled with grapes
bodies looking for shades,
young men chasing young women
rubbing grapes inside their dress
breasts bleeding red
under the light of the moon

jumping up from women for the eye to see
and the hand to reach,
the village was just a large skin
cobblestones without intimacy
sounds with no recall
intimacy as small
as objects with no mystery.

"Wine and milk,"
grandfather said,
"the first habits of intimacy."

The Flap of Your Wings

opened a path of air
for my tired soul
to soar in dreams
through corridors of color lit
by exploding sunrises
and moon-rained fields.

We explored the winds
admiring the easy climb
to the heights
and the vertiginous descent
in the light
changing colors
as you crossed the sun's rays
looking like a bleeding wound
in the center of the sky.

How did you learn to fly
so young?

My soul had found an eagle
to crisscross the sky
with no other ambition
than reach the perfect height
and steal the perfect flight
from the corridors of the moon,
the wind and the sun.

Was this Paradise?

I told you to fly
avoiding the dark spills on the beach
but you wanted to touch
the waves of the sea
and fell in the trap
your body all black

your wings folded
waddling about like a duck.

I'll wait for a wave
to rinse your wings,
but think of the life we miss!

The Witch

She protested innocence
but there was calculation
in her green eyes
and expectation
in her empty smile,

"I can get anyone I want,"
she confessed,

and proceeded to set herself down
in my hands.

It was late autumn,
the scent of her petals
ran the seasons back
to an original garden with dreams
where the magic of her wild seed
grew a rose I stole
in the ambush of her victory.

Suddenly she grew thorns
left my hands and tried to break
the reflections of the rose in my eye,
she had to take what she made
others grow for her.
Too late,
in my garden I control
who lives and who dies.

The victory made the witch return
bent on killing the rose
stepping on the petals of memory
as if they were her own
and not the life I gave the rose
in my soul.

Poor witch!
She will never learn
that it is easier to love
than to overcome
the ambush of victory!

La Chunga

She was once the fire child
of Hemingway dancing to celebrate
the fire of life
well into the night
as if she were the center of the earth
waiting to be split open
into night and day
the fury of life made visible
to the eye in the fire
of her legs and her arms.

Years later she met a friend of mine
who fell in love with her
against the approval of his family
but with the smiles of Spain,
the whole world loved them
on their wedding day.

(Jose Luis, my friend,
was the first man I saw in Spain
carrying money in his trouser pockets
without the protection of a wallet.)

The days of blood and sand were over,
how could the sun fray,
a rose fade,
give the memory of scent
but retain the fire, and dance
flamenco with the rhythm of Tai Chi?

To day in Café de Chinitas
memories weighed like rain
from a summer storm,
she was no longer married to my friend,
she hated the socialists,
she felt pain and aches,

she sat with my hands in hers,
she cried and let go of my hands
begging me to leave.

Gypsies only stood on the eves.

I Share My Bed

with two women
in the same skin,
I chose one,
the other chose me,
the two never meet.

I remember the day of my choice
and the light of that hour
when ready to call the whole thing off
she wore a blue dress
and her blue eyes
stole my body away
to where sky and sea meet,
the world stood still
my body reached
the horizons of the flesh,
not in thought, or wish,
but with the sensations of skin
and the guarantee
of equal proportions of feeling
if I kept her near me,
which I did.

She did not seem aware
of the way her image
entered my soul
and struggled on her own
day by day
to taste her own life
in unknown proportions
of anger and discontent,
an excess of external stimulation
killing time
until her body could reach
the same limits as mine.

In time her frame became wider
than her empirical self,

she shrank while I learned
to live with my eyes closed
not knowing if it was herself
or the image of myself
she was trying to discard!

The Women of Five Continents

one act, one hundred,
it was all the same:
the scramble for the gate,
the forced exit
into the dark.
Another woman, another act,
another turn of the revolving
door, loneliness at dawn.
Eyes, lips, thighs multiply
and the night goes on,
the body bent in surrender,
another act,
the cry of contentment,
the return of another night,
the exit into the light
burying memories to begin
once more. Was it a beginning?
Was it an end?
It was all the same.
Until she came:
only one act held to the light,
no nights, no dawns, no clocks
counting the times but a return
to the starting gate of the gods
to the beginning with no ends,
darkness leading to light,
the inside of the gate.

No, it is not the same.

The Nightclub

A recurring nightmare,

a large room, tall, black walls,
lavender drapes, a door
to the right of the stage
letting red heat and light
filter through
the throbbing heart of a sun
with the fury of a pack
of bulldogs with rabies,
and the sudden fear
the steps backwards in the dark
through the narrow corridor
and the sweat over the whole body
as I wake up.

I would have forgotten this dream
the way I had forgotten others
had not my friends taken me
to that nightclub my first night
in Tokyo.

I knew at once I had been there before,
I could with my eyes closed
find each corner and hidden door,
and the dream came to me.

I quickly forgot the people at the bar
on the dance floor
and moved by the tall walls
and lavender drapes to the door
I feared in my dream,
it looked so ordinary, so innocent,
a door with no secrets within.

It opened
and women filed past me
beautiful women in red

scantilly dressed
I would have sat with them
at a table and danced
except they all looked
vaguely familiar,
women in my past
women I had loved and left
or been left by them,
why were they as young
as when I knew them?

I stood within the frame of the door
the room was black and red
except for the woman at the center
standing up with her back turned,
she was also so young,
she held her back in a silence
more loud than the noise
in the large room
she turned around
to talk without curiosity
or hesitation:

"O, it's you!" She held my eyes.

"This is the time.
You are busy now. Why don't I come back
tomorrow morning at nine?"

There was a long pause, she laughed,
she looked so beautiful,
her eyes flashed a thousand signals
of light that might have reached me,
but her laugh was so dry, so cold,
it felt like a tornado in the soul,
the sudden excitement
and the total devastation.

"Playboy . . ."

"Madam . . ."

Why did we sound as
if delivering lines from a script?
Were we part of a scheme?

"Tomorrow at nine!" She turned her back.

I had a whole night to get ready.
I was not curious, nor afraid,
it felt as if I were in a play
except I did not know my part
nor the end.

I Threw Them Out

The pain had been so intense
I asked them all
to leave,
and so they did,
the good and the bad angels
after a whole night
of fighting.

Very soon the house
felt empty,
the lights had no walls,
no ceiling, no floor,
the wind could turn
no corners and the fog
slithered across
with no furniture to cling to,

it was the life of ghosts
giving me the same cold
they give the stones
in the cemetery.

The Fear of the Same

placed their naked bodies
within that motel
a roaring sea to their faces
a noisy road
at their backs
their bodies the only line
separating the vast spaces
of the sound and view of water
from the roaring trucks
and maids trying to clean back
the dust of centuries;
two bodies trapped
like linen on a clothesline
determined to make love

a woman and a man
between a beach
and a ditch
on a bed with paper thin
walls forced
to protect their intimacy
with towels on the windows
instead of curtains,

but the heart was determined
to consummate an act of love
in the only space left to them
by a world cursed with the rush
to drive the same road
fish on the same beach
shorten the time
to be in company
and kiss out of silence
the images of the deep
desires of the heart
in their struggle
to live or die

with other or alone
in a ditch by the wayside.

It was a short space left,
a woman's body in length
as much space as any warrior
needs to live or die

as their lips meet
resting on each other's weight
at a point of flesh
held and lightly pressed
until the point changes
from skin to liquid heat

and voices from distant waters
rush from under gates of stone
mist and fog
hypnotized by the rising dawn
within the field of flesh
a space crying for the colors of the gods
the earth suddenly transformed
into fire within rising air
as water on water races
to the crest of the mouth
and climbs over a threshold of mortals
to a sea where humans empty each other
of all the dust hidden
under the mounds of their names,

and they emptied themselves of themselves
as they built a world
they could not call by their name
for it became the face
of the cycles of the light
witnessing its own return
to the mirror where the gods
watch their own face
and where lovers trace
the image of their desire

to the light willing
its own act of love.

By the wayside the world
continues to fish and drive,
the light is more
and the noise distant.

What Mask Shall We Wear Today?

Where did you hide
as we made love?
Through my hands you filtered,
a ghost of a thousand caves:

Neither male, nor female, nor hermaphrodite,
neither virgin, woman, old or young,
neither chaste, harlot, shy,
but all of them at once!

It was not I who killed all of you
through poison, famine or sword,
I laid on you my empty hands
and each left by a mysterious death,
but where?

Heaven, earth, fire, sea?
You were everywhere,
in neither of them
and in all at once!

I chased the flight of your breath
to the seed of our origin,
not of husband, lover, relative, friend,
nor servant, master, hired hand,
but all at once!

Neither of pyramid, tomb, or stone
but a tree raised upon a grave
without a corpse . . .

Love grows upon graves!

What mask shall we wear today?

I Had Never Learned to Handle

fire, air or water
but stole them from
eyes, faces and dreams
and burned the plot of land
any woman offered as home,

it was a simple dream
that of turning earth to water
and climb its crest
to the waves of air in the sky
and descend as fire
to let new water rise
from the moisture of the earth,

and carry the earth with me,

only the earth was dry
or I burned it prolonging my stay
or drowned in the waters by the gate,

but it was not a dream
for my life is joined
to the waves of air
rising from the moisture
of your cave
as we carry fire
all the way to the sky
and descend to your same earth
in an unending flight
of earth to water to air to fire
to the light that joins us
to the same play
gods and angels play
when they descend
and embrace the moisture
of the earth.

The Friend

I kissed you on the cheeks
with open eyes,
a brush of the lips
and you stayed outside
where we kissed.
But today I close my eyes
slow my pace
our bodies touch
and you stay with me
inside.
Next time we meet
I know I will lower my eyes
afraid the one inside
might not recognize my friend.

In the Cemetery

In the cemetery of love
there are two graves
I never wanted to visit:
the father who abandoned
his daughter
to be raised by another
and the daughter of
that same father
who abandons
the love she
brings to birth.
Bad blood runs
under the graves.

Hanging Gardens

I am not of the sky or the earth
I inhabit the mid-region
a place I have to invent
with the task, the language,
the social rules
and the rules of intimacy,
if I catch myself remembering
it is time to move.

But you, woman, may stay,
make a home in this hanging garden
as long as you don't claim
to be the only season,
the only flower, the leaf
to let the sun shine
or the bird sing,

this is the place for those
who share equal proportions
of forgetfulness,

those who still remember themselves
live on the earth
or hope for the sky
a sure sign their present world
is already dead.

You and I need to hang our souls
from these hanging gardens
and seed the skies with their roots
and bury their branches in the earth.

The Gods Must Have Laughed

the day we signed
our life contract,
the devils must have taken a nap
for all knew I would be wax
in your Anglo-Saxon hands,

soon enough you stole my land
claiming to make it a home
and buried all my gods
with the familiar spots of my past,

you filled the empty spaces
with faces with no memory
to me or the corners you filled
until you stole the home of my soul,

you exchanged my will of centuries
by your whim of laboring work
a maniac damnation to measure space
by the quantities it held,
I was condemned to become a recluse
in my own basement
by candlelight
having to invent
the path back to the sun,

I jumped the first hurdle of the dark
paying bill of things
I never learned the name
—necessities or bargains—
chains of a cluttered soul
with no limits to what it can hold,

horses, boats, flowers, clothes,
a grocery list my soul could not keep
buried by the musty taste
of my Tower of London
with no escape,

I wrote books till my soul ached
closing the gates of my senses
to the cluttered world
you made me hate,
except you asked me to become a handyman
a slave to do to the earth
whatever whim your tongue improvised,
domestication or war
of two cultures in one home?

The gods stopped laughing
and the devils became alert,
you had shaped my soul
in the discipline of a forge
making me as strong
as those old Titans,

it did not matter anymore,
we gave joint birth
to a new child:
the whiteness of your skin,
the blue colors of your sea,
the green of your fields,
a smile with no fog or mist,

and her soul rides from the inside out
on the crest of the last lines
of a horizon visible only to eyes
trained in the paths of the light.

I pray, upon this empty bed,
that she is loved as you are,
loves as I do!

O, My Little Heart

bent on the act of love!
If you want to cry
borrow the sea for eyes!

When I Die

When I die
do not try to cover
my naked acts
with the silky robes
of a hero
or a rogue
or both.
Look inside
and remember instead
that act or that day
when in my company
you said:
"This must be love."

You Were an Icon

of my head,
I kept you at arms' length
as the last ace fate had dealt,
the last step on a ladder of descent,
the life vest for a last storm,

I had to come upon you with my hands
in the innocence of the dark
and claim with each touch every inch
of virgin territory
before I could tell myself
you were not a repetition
or a habit half awake.

You have become the gate to a new life
you and I can now open paths
of water, air, fire
and travel without fear of the return,
at last the hand is free
to feel love without earth.

The Angel of Death

He could feel the deep presence
of her eyes with his back turned
as he moved around the room
talking to anyone
moving in circles to avoid them
but inevitably they would find him,
the room would then disappear
their two bodies joining the distance
with a raw cry of the soul,
—was he the fire or just a moth?

She was an important wife
a land off-limits to a diplomat
so young so beautiful such power
in her eyes as they pierced him
before he leaned to kiss her hand
they held a seriousness that found
a serious space within him.

He could not see the way
to close out that intimacy,
both were held by the same hand
that deals out destiny
with no place to hide
no corner to turn
no time for a rope trick
and make the feeling disappear.

On the last day of her stay
she asked him to meet her
alone at the crematorium
outside the gate of New Delhi
at five in the morning.
How clever, he thought,
no sane person would join them
in the adventure.

It was impossible to sleep
to stop fantasy from running
in and out of intimacy
and ignore the sound of the human heart
on the verge of destruction
or complete calm.
How close can a man get to death?

Two separate cars,
a woman, a man,
the gates of Smashana
the Hindu shelter of the dead
protected by the Lord Shiva,
the exchange of the company of the living
for the silence of the dead
hand in hand
except that the dead were not silent
but bellowed their song of death.

She noticed his hesitation
and pulled him by the hand
deeper into the thickness
of a flame all around them
a combination of rising sun
burning rainbows
and mounds of prostrated dead
spouting fire around their bodies
with the exultation of death.

The landscape disappeared
behind a mist a shimmering waves
warm air transforming the lines
of the outside into the inside
of a red rose
her eyes the only direction
for the soul
as life exploded
cancelling all memory
and broke into a dance
of light and fire

running through their bodies
in rivers of molten lava
joining the burning flesh
into a single landscape
in slow movement first
and then the speed of spinning wheels
with all the axles turning the rims
within her stomach
to mark a path of living light
through her mouth and her thighs,
a circle of fire
giving birth in the spokes
to tiny dwarfs of different colors,
dancing daggers of light
and joy and pain
piercing the joined bodies
to dance upwards to the skies
and down in successive ladders of joy
visible creatures in bodily form
smiling diamond eyes
features formed as soon
as they were released
from the bonds of flesh and bones
eager to play the game
of circling the flesh,
the sun, the rainbows, the fire
bringing life out of death . . .

Suddenly her body rests
on a stone
black with ashes
that fall on the procession
of whirling life and death
penetrating through her
again and again
as if the crematorium had come
to life for judgment day . . .

The sun reached the top of the sky
and the mounds of fire
were no more than embers

covering with the smell
of charred flesh the whole world.

They did not talk
but walked to their separate cars
avoiding the hands
and did not see each other again
until she took her plane.
Only then she looked at him
and cried.

IV
OF THE FIRE

The Womb

Friction of stone
with fire
and human life swims
in a womb of water.

Imagination builds
from the darkness of the deep
synchronic moves
against the softness of walls
protecting two human bodies
from the harm of unity,

life cradled by water
from dot of life
to human form and shape
repeating in memory
a neural chain
with the exact set
of limbs, fingers,
the sketch of a head,
the marks of a face,
eyes, ears, and a neck
floating unrestrained
on a body formed
by the tactile habits
of centuries,
the caress of the walls
within a woman's womb,
the choice
to become human life
and stop
floating in space
without name or home.

Silence
makes it so soft,
so tender, so slow
to move, rock, wave,

listen to the world outside,
noise with no water around,
one more touch,
one more move,
one more jump
before leaving for
the world of air
and starting to cry.

Is the womb
the original Paradise?
Is there
a path back?

I Was Not Born in America

yet America bore me
with the rhythm of its language
and women as company,
manicured lawns leading to walls
as impregnable as my own.

I no longer need a patch of land
with the footprints of my birth
I am content with the outer gates
the ready smile, the use of first names,

acts that keep the soul alive
without the need of proximity
the kudos of social grades
or the revelation of an empty church.

Flowers grow on public lawns
within reach of a hand
sex in the shape of denims
faces or gates
without the barricades of biography.

Why dare break through walls
not knowing if there is a garden
or a home inside
when no one cares for the difference?

O, America, and the young women!

The Philosopher's Stone

(*Maieri Atalanta Fugiens,* EMBLEMA xxi)

Out of a woman and the sea
fac circulum;
draw inside a quadrangle;
and within it a triangle;
fac circulum, again;
you hold now in your hand
lapidem philosophorum.

O Marvel, This Flame in the Garden!

The flowers have learned
to follow the trail of the sun,
flowers grow, flowers die
and only the path remains

not the cause of their life or death
but the flame in the seed
feeding desire for the light
jumping from soul to soul
original markings
of the beginnings and the ends
the light of all shape and form
never to be destroyed
by the salamander or the rose.

I have followed this flame in the garden
through all the mountain paths
forcing the stars to bend their light
at the knees of my flame
up and down a road
lit only by the flame of this garden.

O flame!
I am nearer to you
than you are to yourself,
I am the breath
of the body you needed
to know your own presence!

I Saw the Secret of the Temple

before it could escape:
a flame trailing her body
like a shadow a tree,
the woman stays!

If You put my soul to death,
if You poison all my dreams,
if You return my body to the dust
not to rise as water or air,
if You refuse me your love
by removing her,

remember it is You who dies
and it is You put to death,
and You the poison of my dreams
and You wasting life
by returning my dust to the dust,

for even if You refuse me love
You have given me light
to see You in death, poison,
dust and wasted lives,
not the forms and the shapes,
nor the light I see,
but the light with which I see,
of which the rest is only
a bent image.

And so the woman stays,
for in her I saw the secret
of the Temple before it could escape!

An Angel's Breath on an Empty Mirror

I have seen corpses come to life
with the fire stolen from the hands
of the gods within frames
of mortal earth,

and watched their feet sink in the mud
when others stole their fire
or they forgot to race
the path of the light.

They do not cry in pain
but for the weight
of their stone wings
held down by the air
forced to lie next to each other
plotting ways to climb again.

They are not aware of their own birth
nor do they live in the temple of fire
their life is a game of colors
and the quiver of leaves in the wind.

They do not know themselves,
their shape is not their shape,
their fire remains hidden in a cave,
only those who have seen it before
see it reappear.

Their death is not their death
but the passage of the flame
through shapes and forms
to return with new names
to its home in the clay.

Every name is three
within the clay,
a flash of light,
a breath of life

in two mirrors,
love in search of itself.

Angels only are present at this secret birth
for the original Flame
cannot be born without them
and both share the same origin,
earlier than a mother's womb,

for such a small body of clay
is the home of the flame
a birth in the beginning
and at the end,
the same seed repeated by the Angel
in the birth of the clay,

but no one can be born
not killing their own mother at birth,
though killing her will force
to be born through the same gate
the way of their own death,
the way of their origin,

for life is only death,
life and death the corpse of the Angel,
and being born is being pronounced dead,
for earlier is the Angel
than the birth of the light
we see, for they share the power
to chose our own parents
through new births,

and the gods love them
and conspire with them
to bring all life
through the paths of the light
for they recycle with our birth
the same earth of our clay
until the gods see in it
the light of their own reflection.

Lotus Flower and Sun

synchronized to a game of love,
blossoms resting
in the absence of sun rays
opening up in slow surrender
from a center of moisture and blood
wide as the sun
as it reaches the top of the sky
when sun and flower make visible
the face and the shape of love,

blossoms close again
as the sun descends
to hide from curious eyes
and rest beyond the lake.

My soul, mouth and lips
have at last become synchronized
to the light and rhythm
of this natural hymn,

O, at last
to be known as one is!

The Sound of One Hand

A whole life wasted
digging the earth
for a short cut to the sky,
I piled up bones and dirt,
I would have died
but for a broken glass
that shaped tears
into shining stars.

I buried that stupid man
under the pile of dirt
I dug!

The Interpretation of Dreams

If, under the cover of dreams,
God speaks on Mount Fuji
the Zen Master praises the heavens
for irrigating the garden
while asleep,
then he sits and enjoys the coolness
of the green countryside.

But on Mount Moirah
Abraham packs a donkey
and a knife and takes his son
to be sacrificed
but for the timely arrival
of an angel who holds his hand
and exchanges the son for a ram.

God never spoke again to Abraham
he sent his angels instead,
while fresh rivers still bend
beneath the green thighs
of Mount Fuji
under the rain.

Good Angels

break in
like soft rain
expanding the soul to feeling
larger than the landscape
intimate and tender
like young skin
turning grass, colors, rocks
into dancing waves
of a calm sea
red on mauve and mauve on rocks
and rocks into waves of air
running through the throat
into intimate surrender
in the deepest chamber
of body and soul
joined into a world of feeling
with no noise
only the voice of certainty
that God has lost
his infinite distance.

And the same at play
the sudden change of the world outside
for the silence within
a coincidence of playing field
and playing body
other players marked to receive
the ball once, twice, three times
with complete accuracy
and as much time
as in a race of turtles
and the certainty that
one last move one more turn
and the shot to the goal would score
and it does
such softness
such silence broken with the roar

of the crowd following the external
magical play.

And the look of a beautiful face
a woman without the colors of fashion
but the glow from the inside
as she closes her eyes
and invites intimacy to open wide
with the certainty that behind the gates
she holds the fields of Paradise
the soul stretches to the confines
of intimacy and the silence of the stars
and the touch of all the fingers
of the body of life.

They break in so softly
always from the inside,
in light, slow motion
and the sound of silence,
how can we mistake them
for the bad angels,
our own thoughts
or the sensations from outside?

The Gypsies

The gods who were once mortals
have joined the company of horses,
cows, the shadow of caravans

and the exact music of the stars
as they fashion the movement
of the earth with the sound of drums

to make parents young again
and rise with the flight of cranes
and descend with the softness of rain.

They know the measures by which
the earth and the sky came apart
and their music brings them back

to the sounding silence of chaos,
its divided unity
into the reflection of the light.

They stand at the four corners of the world
singing songs and selling horses
inviting the soul to regather the fragments
and be young again.

The Messenger

"Mary, I am an angel
and you are chosen by God
to carry within you
the seed of his descendants,
you are pregnant by this word,
the mother of a race
that will walk on the lanes
of a new thruway
leading to salvation,
you are the birth of the immanent God,
the womb of a new faith
visible only to those
with eyes that can see
your son contiguous to his Father
in heaven and within
the smallest things on this earth,
you are the fire and light
at the foundations
of a changing world
no longer controlled by fate
but by the direction
of the will of God."

"But how can this be?
I know no man,
and I am engaged!"

"Have faith!"

"Let it be done
as you say!"

"Joseph, wake up!
I am an angel,
your wife is pregnant by the Lord.
Keep her in your home.
Ask no questions,
do as you are told!"

And so it was.
And for many years
women and men
let their souls rest
on the promise of an angel
to a young girl,
and a sleepy old man.

Teresa de Avila

I measured my life
in thimbles of love
squeezed from the memory
of Sunday preachers
as I moved their images about
in my mind
even at times
when I was praying
to You

> *Love of man*
> *in a woman's measure.*

Then I learned to measure it
in cups, as You came to me
in portions of
sky,
water,
fields
quieting my soul
like a pond
still with memories of
summer,
winter,
autumn,
spring,
all I had to do
was to turn my soul face up
like a mirror.

> *Love of the world*
> *in a woman's measure.*

Finally
You came to stop all measure
in the form of an angel,
the body of a man
the face like a flame
carrying in your hand
a dart of gold

the tip all red with fire,
and You
caressed my heart with it
penetrating inside
and would not let go
until all my body
was as red as the fire
penetrating through my heart,
the pain was so deep
it made me groan,
I heard myself moan
for the pain never to stop
but plunge me deep
into that bottomless sea
where at last I could feel
the exact measure
of my woman's desires.

> *Desire of the world,*
> *love for men,*
> *love of God*
> *at last joined*
> *within a woman's measure.*

The Wrestling Angel

I

Our host lived in a castle
protected like a nest
in a valley between Katmandu and Lhasa
as green as an emerald in summer
when the caravans of scientists
trekked up the mountains
collecting the musk
of Himalayan goats.

Water flowed, birds flew,
people talked within an air so clean
they seemed to move in whispers
at the feet of a giant god
reaching from the earth to the sky
in a majestic shawl of snow
the palace an altar
where people live so close
that privacy gives way
to thoughtless innocence.

Tara was the youngest
of the seven daughters of our host
she had grown holding my hand
from a child to a woman
teaching me the names of birds,
how to read the signs in the clouds,
how the people were trained
in the martial arts,
how the shepherdesses in the mountains
could take on any man in a fight
and only surrender to them
if they won, the women never lost,
while I wondered how she had stolen
the emerald green for her eyes,
the softness of lines for her face,
the surging foam of the sky for her soul,
the red flowers for her lips,

the determination of thunder for her will
domesticating the English language
to sound like the breeze.

II

The last time I visited my host
I was on my own,
musk had already been born
in a laboratory,
but it was my habit of summer
and there was Tara,
that summer she was eighteen.

I know altitude makes things look different
but she was the most beautiful woman
I had ever seen even in memory,
(did she have the beauty I missed
in all the other women down below?)
We traveled the same spots of the past,
she did not hold my hand,
she backed me against a cascading river
and ordered me to wrestle her.
She was now a woman she said
and I said yes

She chose the Hall of Mirrors
for the fight,
candles were lit
by servants at the foot of the glass,
the Hall felt as intimate as a giant womb,
the rules were simple
no blows, no blood, a continuous fight.

The women of the palace accompanied her
dressed in a white kimono
with a sash around her waist,
I wore silk pajamas
her father was my best man.

A gong signaled the start of the fight,
we came to the center of the mat and bowed,
there were no smiles on her face,
we returned to our corners
a second gong signaled the start,
suddenly I realized where I was,
looked at the candles, the mirrors, too late,
she got hold of my arm,
turned me over her shoulder
and I was on the floor,
there were giggles all around,
I saw a hundred red faces, my own,
staring at me from the walls,
I got up and rushed to her
flailing my arms in the air
to find my body spun around
to the edge of the ring
(I was not ready for her,
she was going to win,
win, lose, was this a game?).

I took a deep breath and waited
for her to come to me,
we stalked each other
and came close enough
to look into each other's eyes,
the whole Hall and the candles
were burning inside,
a split second of distraction
and I was again on the floor,
she was better at reading me
than I at reading her
I had to concentrate more on the game,

I lowered my eyes, caught her rising leg
and lifted it until she lost her balance
then I moved away,
there was silence,
only the air of our lungs
rushed through the teeth

and the held cry of breath
against the contact on the charge,
I knew I had her now,
I pinned her to the ground
using her clothes as a knot
to cross her arms against the floor,
I began to smile,

She escaped naked from under my hands,
a bundle of clothes
my eyes bulging out of my head
her naked body and the thousand reflections
of her on the walls,
she spun around on her left foot
once, twice, three times she slapped
my throat with her right foot
I stumbled backwards and fell on my back
she stood on top ready to strike,
I waited for the foot to rise
threw her backwards with a twist,
she hissed, her body arched
and shot herself against me
her foot found a perfect target
on my chest
she held herself while I found my breath,

she came at me, lifted me by my clothes
and ripped them in one single motion,
as she threw them to the side
the audience filed out of the Hall
and we were alone.

Many candles died
before I learned the game
of neither winning or losing
but concentrating in the play
the way snow plays with rain
and water with the earth
forcing rivers down the mountain
softening the bed of rocks
caressing the foot of trees

climbing the grass to bring life
to the sleeping hills
riding the length of the earth
the way she rode my flesh
from head to feet with no human stops
or she would push me with her feet
against the wall.

We covered that night
the length of a thousand fields
climbed the top of the mountain
to the starting gate
and flowed like a stream
down the slopes until the body
became as wide and soft as the sea.
It was then that the seasons
flowed together as one,
spring, summer, autumn, winter,
earth, water, fire, air
fused in one body
a totality of sensation
that even the earth
has to stagger not to explode,
fire on fire, water on water,
air on air, soil on soil,
water against rock,
heat melting ice at the top
to bring together as one
the cry of victory
and surrender of a man and a woman
at war.

White and green light
made a ladder of flesh
from the heavens to the earth
and back where all ladders start:
in the wrestling game for love
with no goals, no ends.

The sun broke through the window,
outside a red flower had grown

that night over the snow on the mountain,
the eye caught only the red on white,
inside, the Hall mirrors reflected
the red flower in every wall,
the woman smiled!

(It's that smile I remember.
Have I already lived my life
while plucking flowers
one by one?)

I Have Learned

in your presence
to read the signs of the soul
accustomed as I was to season
after season of storms
and the derangement of the senses.

With you I have learned to see
the line that marks
peace from storm
feel the silence of
the light in the morning
lifting sleep
from the habits of ages
and raise my face to the caresses
of the soft rain.

I can separate now
drops falling on a sponge
from the splash of water on stone
moments condemned to stay or die
images alive and those with no trail
or desire to recall a face or a name.

You alone stay in company
and mark the hours of a world
of deep feeling that links
the soul to a sea of souls
who learned to love
from the inside.

Only angels and gods love
with such soft touch!

It Was Easy

to steal
the visible lines of a face
the colors and size of eyes
the touch and softness of skin
and build bridges of fantasy
into dreamt regions of intimacy

but lines are just lines
and colors are just colors
and skin is just skin
and fantasy builds only
the mist of dreams
upon the sand of make-believe.

But how steal your intimacy
and cross the invisible line
that eyes, colors, skin
only hide?

You sat by my side
—it was so simple—
and led my hand to touch
with closed eyes
the covered space
between breasts and thighs

my hand felt the softness and depth
of clouds parting
to let the sun shoot arrows
of burning flames up my arm
and burn my unsuspected insides,
thousand tongues of burning air
caressing my soul
in successive waves
of fire on fire
until I forgot
the earth, the water and even
the riding air

to become one flame
with the fire up there
and down within.

I am no longer cluttered
by the proximity of things
I can look them in the face
and see our common intimacy!

The Majestic Flight of the Eagle

harnessing wings to soar
from the side of the mountain
to the rocks at the crest of the horizon
and avoid a life in reverse
down a spiral of descent

if only we keep memory free
and hold our flight on a wave of air
and train our eyes to separate
skin from feathers
and descend as lightning

to steal from every cave
the nectar of the gods
with the same accuracy
the same exact measure
as two eagles mate in midair

controlled free fall
through walls of air
two bodies joined
in the celebration of life
coming apart
before they hit
the secure spots
of the lamb and the ox,

there is no other flight
for the soul!

One Single Nest

Sky and earth race
towards each other
the rain extends its arms
to seal the light of the world
within their embrace

a man and a woman left
to cuddle on a lonely bed
as the last light is drained
their blind hands grope in the dark
the black eyes of the woman
look at the man
desire of the flesh at bay
as the flesh waits with feline calm
if to pounce or lie
next to the body of the man

and they settle for the contact of the flesh
skin against skin
pore opening to pore
until their bodies break
their own distance
and blend as light straws
into one single flesh.

And so they stay
and out of the two
they make one single nest
as they hold the light of the world.

The Shadows of Emptiness

have found a place in your soul
I saw silent dew drip
under your smiles,
chains of liquid pearls
falling down like polished clouds
darkening the field of your face.
How could I have missed them before?

Fear and hope steal light from the soul,
have you seen the flame
that springs from incense?
Curled rings of sweet smoke
choke the flame to death
with the perfumes of the soul,
tears dirty the soul
as much as virtue and sin.

Let the soul love only with the soul,
let the flame love only the flame
in the flame,
and let the flesh curl
with the rings of smoke,

do not spill your soul
with tears of fear or hope,
let the flame rise on its own!

The Last Day

But it had to be a dream
the way the angel pulled me
by the hair to ride a surf of air
with the same feeling within
as when flesh breaks through flesh,

of late in dreams or awake
I have lost the boundaries
between body and soul
as when we rode
through walls of air
to a mountaintop,

"You are going to watch
the day of judgment."

The empty countryside
gave only peace from inside
i was expecting the earth to shake
and give out in perfect shapes
the bodies of the dead,
those who knew some one
and those no one identified,
legions of men and women
dressed up in linen, perhaps nude,
God did not own the garment district,
old, young, somewhere in between?

The countryside continued empty
except that the breeze gave out
a warmer and deeper feeling
horizons of peace
the soul knew would not be broken.

Who would be the judge?
Angels, God, a computer in the sky?
Where would the shame be?
Who would hear the count

or care to point a finger at anyone?
The eyes and ears of judgment
must be the same
as the eyes and ears that made the choice.
Could God recreate the times,
the place, the details of each deed
so that justice would ring true
in the hearts of the condemned?

"It is time to go," the angel said.

"But no one is here.
Where is the last day?"

We rode again upwards
to a point in mid-space
the warm feeling inside changed
for a body with the temperature
of a frozen icicle,

from above and below
the body was at the center
of two whirling cones
pressing the tips
against the head and loins
boring in and out
the faces of all the dead
flesh through flesh
leaving the soul bruised
but unable to stop,

the body could not stand
fire, water, air, earth
being no longer flame,
drop, wave, speck
but live faces with consciousness
sensuality beyond human flesh
as the whirls penetrated deeper
and multiplied,

speeding, symmetrical cones
tearing the soul
along the rims and the center
begging for death to come
being covered instead
by a wave of light
with the body of ether
shooting flames from below
to become at the top light
tuning the cones to the sound
of the agony of death
and the peace of Paradise,

I knew then the body had to die
riding the music of the light
with the body of ether
moving to embrace the faces
of the rivers of the sky . . .